Alexandrian M.S.
Vatican ms
Sinaitic   ms "   "   " 350 AD.

Iranaus quotes from
Matt 180 — times
  John 80
  acts 50
  Rom 60
  1st Cor. 60?
  2 — 71

Clement of Alexandria quotes from

  mat 400
  mk 80
  Luk 300
  John 240
  acts 110

PROFESSOR GEORGE P. FISHER'S WORKS.

"Topics of profound interest to the studious inquirer after truth are discussed by the author with his characteristic breadth of view, catholicity of judgment, affluence of learning, felicity of illustration, and force of reasoning. . . . His singular candor disarms the prepossessions of his opponents. . . . In these days of pretentious, shallow, and garrulous scholarship, his learning is as noticeable for its solidity as for its compass."

—N. Y. TRIBUNE.

History of the Christian Church. 8vo, with Maps,	$3.50
Supernatural Origin of Christianity. New Edition, Crown 8vo,	2.50
The Reformation. New Edition, Crown 8vo,	2.50
The Beginnings of Christianity. New Edition, Crown 8vo,	2.50
Grounds of Theistic and Christian Belief. Crown 8vo,	2.50
Discussions in History and Theology. 8vo,	3.00
Faith and Rationalism. New Edition, 12mo,	.75
The Christian Religion. New Edition, 16mo,	.50
Manual of Christian Evidences. 16mo,	.75
The Nature and Method of Revelation. 12mo,	1.25
Manual of Natural Theology. 16mo,	.75

MANUAL OF

CHRISTIAN EVIDENCES

BT
1101
F53
1900

MANUAL OF
CHRISTIAN EVIDENCES

BY
GEORGE PARK FISHER, D.D., LL.D.
TITUS STREET PROFESSOR OF ECCLESIASTICAL HISTORY IN YALE UNIVERSITY

NEW YORK
CHARLES SCRIBNER'S SONS
1900

COPYRIGHT, 1888, BY
CHARLES SCRIBNER'S SONS

TROW DIRECTORY
PRINTING AND BOOKBINDING COMPANY
NEW YORK

PREFACE.

The half-formed intention to write a short manual of Christian Evidences, which I had for some time entertained, took a definite form on account of requests coming to me from persons entitled to respect, some of whom were engaged in the practical work of teaching. It appeared to me that a brief book, confining itself to the Evidences of Revealed Religion, and setting forth in a connected form the principal topics of definition and proof, would be useful to readers and to pupils who have not time for the study of more extended treatises.[1]

Paley's Evidences, which was so long the standard text-book on the subject, notwithstanding the signal merits which characterize it, has one striking fault. To the internal evidence a very subordinate place is assigned. The argument for miracles is deprived of

[1] In "The Grounds of Theistic and Christian Belief" (Charles Scribner's Sons, 1883), I have handled the main topics of Natural Theology, and have presented more in detail the proofs of Revelation. In that work, controverted points are discussed more at length.

the legitimate, if not indispensable, advantage which is gained by a preliminary view of the need and the intrinsic excellence of the Christian Revelation. Moreover, the aspects of skepticism and disbelief have somewhat changed since Paley's time. Books like Strauss's "Life of Jesus" had not then been written. Patristic study has also made advances. The proofs from this source require some revision. Besides, Paley's work is too long for the demands of those for whom the present manual is designed.

G. P. F.

New Haven, May 16, 1888.

CONTENTS.

CHAPTER I.

WHAT IS TO BE PROVED AND THE NATURE OF THE EVIDENCE, ... 1

CHAPTER II.

WHAT IS MEANT BY MIRACLES? THE POSSIBILITY OF THEM, AND THE POSSIBILITY OF PROVING THEM, . 9

CHAPTER III.

HOW THE ANTECEDENT PRESUMPTION AGAINST THE OCCURRENCE OF MIRACLES IS SET ASIDE, . . . 21

CHAPTER IV.

ADMITTED FACTS RESPECTING CHRISTIANITY, . . 28

CHAPTER V.

PROOF OF THE SUPERNATURAL ORIGIN OF CHRISTIANITY FROM THE PORTRAITURE OF THE CHARACTER OF JESUS IN THE EVANGELISTS, ... 32

CHAPTER VI.

Proof of the Miracles from Peculiar Features of the Gospel Narratives, ... 37

CHAPTER VII.

Proof of the Resurrection of Jesus from Statements by the Apostle Paul, ... 41

CHAPTER VIII.

The Genuineness of the Gospels, ... 47

CHAPTER IX.

Trustworthiness of the Testimony of the Apostles, ... 71

CHAPTER X.

The Proof of the Resurrection of Jesus from the Evangelists, ... 82

CHAPTER XI.

Alleged Errors of the Apostles in Matters of Opinion, ... 86

CHAPTER XII.

Alleged Difficulties in the Connection of Christianity with the Old Testament Religion, . 91

CHAPTER XIII.

Proof of Christianity from Prophecy, . . . 95

CHAPTER XIV.

ARGUMENT FOR CHRISTIANITY FROM THE CONVERSION AND THE CAREER OF THE APOSTLE PAUL, . . 99

CHAPTER XV.

PROOF OF THE DIVINE ORIGIN OF CHRISTIANITY FROM THE INTRINSIC EXCELLENCE OF THE CHRISTIAN SYSTEM, ... 105

CHAPTER XVI.

PROOF AFFORDED BY THE CONTRAST OF CHRISTIANITY WITH OTHER RELIGIONS AND WITH PHILOSOPHICAL SYSTEMS, ... 107

CHAPTER XVII.

CORROBORATIVE PROOF OF THE TRUTH OF CHRISTIANITY FROM ITS UTILITY, ... 114

CHAPTER XVIII.

CORROBORATIVE PROOF OF CHRISTIANITY FROM ITS RAPID SPREAD IN THE FIRST CENTURIES, . . 117

INDEX, ... 121

CHRISTIAN EVIDENCES.

CHAPTER I.

WHAT IS TO BE PROVED AND THE NATURE OF THE EVIDENCE.

The question. The design of this book is to prove that the narratives of the life of Jesus which are contained in the New Testament are true, and that Christianity has a supernatural, divine origin and sanction. Did Christ speak from himself, or was his doctrine "of God" in a sense not to be affirmed of any system of which man alone is the author?[1] Is Christianity, in distinction from other religions, stamped with an authoritative character, as being a revelation from God? If the history of Jesus as it is recorded in the Gospels, and of the planting of the Church as it is described in the Acts and the Epistles, is worthy of belief, these questions must have an affirmative answer.

The subject of the present inquiry should be kept distinctly in view. The purpose is not to prove the

---

[1] —"whether it be of God, or whether I speak from myself," John vii. 17 (Revised Version).

truths of natural religion. The existence of God and the fact of his government of the world are taken for granted. It is true that, through the impression which Christianity makes, one may have his doubts on these fundamental points removed. Christianity, even prior to the examination of its external proofs, may awaken a more clear perception of the being of God, and a more firm and vivid conviction of the free and responsible nature of man, and of the reality of a future life. But great as the quickening and enlightening influence of Revelation may be in this direction, it is the function of Natural Theology to set forth the grounds of theism and what reasons exist for believing man to be immortal. Nor is it our purpose to take up the question of the *inspiration* of the Scriptures—the question whether, and to what extent, the authors of the books of the Bible were aided by the Spirit of God in the composition of them. This is an important topic of theology, but it is not involved in our present undertaking. Nor, once more, is it necessary to inquire whether or not the Gospel narratives are free from discrepancies and like imperfections, such as pertain in some degree to the most trustworthy historical writings. The substantial verity of the New Testament histories is the only point that we are at present called upon to establish. We may illustrate these distinctions.

marginal note: What it is not designed to prove.

John Marshall wrote the Life of Washington. He had personally known Washington and, besides, resorted to authentic documents and to other sources of information. Marshall was an intelligent and upright man. Hence the biography which he composed is substantially accurate. It is conceivable, however, that Washington should have himself read the proof-sheets, and (supposing his own memory to be perfect) have removed all errors, even the most minute, or even that he should have dictated the entire biography, with the exception of the account of his own death. But the author, whether he wrote with these special advantages or not, was so placed as to be qualified to produce a narrative which should be in all its material features correct.

<small>Meaning of "Genuineness" and of "Credibility."</small> In the Evidences of Christianity are included the proofs of the *genuineness* and of the *credibility* of the New Testament writings. A writing is *genuine* if it was written by the author to whom it is ascribed. But it is well to remark that a narrative may be *credible*, or *authentic*, even if the ordinary view taken of its authorship is mistaken. If Julius Cæsar's Commentaries, in which he speaks of himself in the third person, were to be found to have been written, not by him, but by an intelligent and truthful Roman officer who was with him through the Gallic wars, or even by some competent person to whom Cæsar had related the facts, that work,

although not *genuine*, would still be *authentic*. Respecting the New Testament histories, the main point to be first established is that they present fairly the testimony of the Apostles, the immediate companions of Jesus. The question of the authorship of these books is important, but that of their date and of other circumstances relating to their origin and early reception, are of more vital consequence.

The proofs of the truth of the Gospel histories are of the same kind as those on which our belief in other historical works is founded.

<small>What is historical evidence?</small>

We require as the warrant for believing in such narratives that they shall rest upon credible testimony of witnesses or well-informed contemporaries. A certain value belongs to tradition—a value varying with the degree of nearness of the events, and in some measure with other circumstances. Moreover, a great many things may serve to corroborate—or else to disprove—historical statements. Occurrences, if they are of a very important character, produce effects upon society in a great many different ways. These effects remain as monuments of the events in which they had their origin. Thus, the great fact of the War of the American Revolution is attested by the existence of the Republic of the United States, and by the character of its institutions, not to dwell on minor consequences, such as the public observances which commemorate the birth of the nation.

NATURE OF THE EVIDENCE.

The evidences of Christianity, like historical proofs generally, are *probable*, as distinguished from *demonstrative*. In the case of demonstrative proof, the opposite of the thing asserted is not only *false;* it is *inconceivable*. This is not true of anything depending on probable or moral evidence. There are *degrees* of probability. Thus we say of one thing that it is "slightly probable;" of another, that it is "very probable;" and of a third, that it is "extremely," or "in the highest degree" probable. It should be observed, however, that in numberless cases where the evidence is of the kind termed "probable," we are absolutely free from doubt. We may never have seen London, but we have not a whit more doubt that London exists than we have that the sum of the three angles of a triangle is equal to two right angles. We never saw Napoleon the First, but we are not less certain that Napoleon lived than we are that two parallel lines, however prolonged, will never meet. To entertain a doubt on the one proposition would be as decisive a proof of insanity as to entertain a doubt on the other.

Nature of probable evidence.

The proofs of Christianity are *cumulative*. This is a circumstance which inquirers and disputants are very apt to overlook. In regard to all the main propositions involved in the case, the evidence is made up of many particulars,

The evidence cumulative.

all together pointing to the same conclusion. Under this head there are two mistakes to be avoided. One consists in demanding a demonstration for each item in the evidence, where, in the nature of things, no demonstration is possible. The other mistake, which is hardly less grave, is in isolating each particular of proof, as if it stood by itself. It is the old error of assuming that because a single rod may perchance be broken, the whole bundle is equally fragile.

The proofs of Christianity are either *internal*, or *external*. The external evidence is the testimony,

<small>"External" and "Internal" Evidence.</small> simply considered, to the facts which are related in the Gospels. The internal evidence includes everything in the system of Christianity itself which is adapted to inspire faith in its truth and divine origin. "Christianity is founded upon certain great primary wants and affections of the human soul, which it meets, to which it corresponds, and of which it furnishes the proper objects and satisfactions. There is the feeling after a God; there is the instinct of prayer; there is conscience and the sense of sin; there is the longing for and dim expectation of immortality. Christianity supplies the counterpart of these affections and wants of the soul, and it is as supplying this counterpart that it recommends itself in the first instance to us; it appeals to our belief upon the strength of its own characteristics, at the same

time that it comes before us as a subject of external evidence. The nature of Christianity, and its correspondence to our own nature, has a legitimate influence upon our minds, before any other consideration; it is one part of the whole Christian evidence, and a valid and necessary part, without which the other, or the historical proof, is reasonably and logically deficient."[1]

It will be generally acknowledged that for the due appreciation of the evidences of Revelation, earnest attention and a candid temper are requisite. It must be added that the affections form one element in determining the judgment. On other subjects it is true that the data for a judgment must be drawn in part from other sources than the understanding. It is plain that in deciding questions in the fine arts—such as the genuineness of a painting or the merit of a piece of music—a sympathetic tact, native or acquired, is demanded. The like is true respecting questions where the moral excellence, whether of teaching or of personal character, is involved. The evidence is made up in part of impressions, and these depend on the inward state of the person who is to pass judgment. "We cannot possibly enter deeply into character without affections; we cannot estimate or comprehend truly, we cannot embrace keenly and with a living force, what is beautiful,

The affections as a source of proof.

[1] J. B. Mozley's Lectures and other Theological Papers, p. 3.

profound, and touching in the mind and disposition of any person of extraordinary goodness, unless there are affections in us which enable us to seize hold of their moral traits, and inspire us with a vivid admiration and appreciation of them."[1] In all such cases, when one is confronted with moral evidence, there is a probation of character.

[1] Ibid., page 8.

CHAPTER II.

WHAT IS MEANT BY MIRACLES? THE POSSIBILITY OF THEM, AND THE POSSIBILITY OF PROVING THEM.

The most common objection both to the genuineness and the credibility of the New Testament histories is from the accounts of miracles, which they contain. It is expedient, at the outset, to consider what weight belongs to this objection, and also to determine what place should be assigned to miracles among the proofs of revelation.

What is a miracle? A miracle is an event which *Definition of a miracle.* the forces of nature—including the natural powers of man—cannot of themselves produce, and which must, therefore, be referred to a supernatural agency. Or, in the briefer phrase of Pascal, a miracle is an event exceeding the natural power of the means employed. If the event is of such a character, or takes place under such circumstances, as to exclude the supposition of a superhuman created agent as its cause, then it must be inferred that God is its author. It should be added, to complete the idea of a miracle, that it is something manifest—something that can be known and apprehended by men. There is a course of nature—a natural order—the same antecedents being followed by the same consequents. This order of succession we call the uniformity of nature. It enables us, on the ground of previous observation, to predict what will occur. In an atmosphere of 32° Fahrenheit water will freeze. In a warmer atmosphere it will remain fluid. A body of less specific gravity than the air will rise; a body of greater specific gravity than the air will fall. A deviation in any instance from this order of sequences is what is meant by a miracle. But to fill out the ordinary signification of the word, the fact must occur in connection with religious teaching, or as a verification of the claim of a religious teacher to a divine commission. In the New Testament, three terms are used to denote miracles. They are called "wonders," primarily in reference to the astonishment which they produce; "powers," as related to the divine energy to which they are due; and "signs," or tokens of God's presence and of the sanction thus afforded to the teacher or to what is taught.[1]

New Testament terms.

It is contended by some that a miracle is impossible; by others that, even if it be not impossible, it can never be proved.

---

[1] For example: "Signs and wonders" (John iv. 48); "powers" (Matt. xi. 20, Revised Version, in the margin). The rendering of the original word (found in Matt. xi. 20, etc.) is usually "mighty works."

1. It is said that an event not produced by natural laws would be an event without a cause. But what is natural law? By natural law is simply meant the method of the action of natural forces. Laws are another name for the established sequences—that is, the customary succession—of natural phenomena. *When a miracle occurs, a new cause intervenes*—viz., a special exertion of divine power, the power of the Creator and Upholder of nature. There is not even a violation of natural laws, in the proper sense of the phrase; for every statement of natural law, and every prediction of what is to occur under it, are made with the *proviso*, or on the tacit supposition, that there is to be no intervention of a supernatural agent. A miracle nowise contradicts the axiom that in nature the same causes, under the same circumstances, are followed by the same effects. In the case of a miracle, the effect is different because the causes are not the same. The variation in the effect is what must take place, supposing such an alteration of the antecedents. If a new cause comes in, it is irrational to look for the same effect as before.

As we pass from one kingdom of nature to another, we find that higher forces control the action of lower, so that new effects are produced which could not otherwise occur. Inorganic nature in this way is subject to vital forces. The force of

Marginal note: Not an event without a cause.

gravitation, for example, gives way under the action of a superior agency of another kind. Out of the seed rises the stalk of the plant. If we had no knowledge of organic nature, we might be led to deny the possibility of such a fact as the movement upward of a growing tree, despite the force of gravitation.

<small>Forces overcome by forces in nature.</small>

The human will affords the most striking illustration of the possibility of a miracle. The will, as related to material forces, is a distinct and higher power, and as thus related is supernatural. *It initiates movements in the realm of nature.* It produces results—countless in number and variety—which would not have come into being independently of its action. When a boy throws a ball into the air, gravitation is overcome by forces set in motion by a human volition. Whoever bakes a loaf of bread brings into being a thing which the bare forces of nature, not controlled and assisted by man's will, could not have produced. In this way human will-power creates all that goes under the comprehensive name of *art*. From the least motion of a finger, in obedience to volition, to the most complex contrivances of mechanical genius, from the building of a wigwam to the erection of a Gothic cathedral, from the management of a village-school to the leading of armies and the government of nations—in a word, wherever the effects of

<small>The human will, supernatural.</small>

human will appear, there are beheld phenomena which the laws of nature—apart from the guidance, combination, and control of them by man's will—could never have brought into being. A miracle, where there is an interposition of the divine will, is not anti-natural, but super-natural.

2. But it is objected that the invariability of nature—when the human will with its range of activities is included—is a truth which it is absurd to call in question. This objection assumes that the uniformity of nature is intuitively known, is a necessary truth, and stands thus on a level with mathematical axioms. No sound philosopher will make such an assertion. Our belief that the course of things is uniform is based on observation and experience, coupled with an instinctive confidence in the indications—*indicia*—of nature, like the trust which we put in the signs of thought when we are in communication with human beings. A child who has once burned his finger in the flame, knows that if he makes a second experiment of the same sort, the same result will occur. We naturally assume that nature is an orderly system, that it is conformed to a plan, and is not made to deceive us. Our belief in the uniformity of nature justifies a presumption that there will be (and has been) no departure from it. This presumption, however, may be overruled and set aside, wherever reasons exist which would make it

The uniformity of nature.

wise in the Author and Ruler of Nature to intervene.

3. It is objected that a miracle would be a contravention by God of the laws of nature which He has himself established. Even were it so, the laws of nature are not *moral* laws. An interference with them would not involve in itself any moral wrong. The foregoing remarks show how one class of natural forces may counteract and govern the action of another, or the results to be produced by that action. Moreover, Natural Theology teaches that natural laws do not exist for their own sake. The end of material nature is not in itself. A "law" is merely a name for the way in which things ordinarily occur. On the supposition that a higher good is to be secured by a deviation from the course of nature, there is no moral objection to such an act on the part of God. If this objection had any weight, it would tend to prove not the *natural*, but only the *moral* impossibility of miracles. But the objection is stripped of its plausibility the moment one admits that there is a moral government of the world as well as an administering of physical laws. Nature is not a thing by itself. It is only one province in the whole divine system. The motives that dictate the establishment and maintenance of the course of nature may require that it should not be absolutely without interruption.

<small>Miracle and natural law.</small>

4. Hume made a celebrated argument against the possibility of proving miracles by testimony, although the same argument had long before been stated and answered in one of South's sermons.[1] Our belief in the uniformity of nature, Hume said, rests on experience. Our belief in testimony has the same foundation. But the experience of the uniformity of nature is without any exception; whereas, we have had experience of the error of human testimony. Hence he concluded that no amount of testimony could prove a miracle; for, if we suppose the amount of evidence of this sort to be never so great, still the supposition of its falsehood would imply at most nothing greater than a miracle, and so we should have a miracle to balance a miracle.

Hume's argument.

Hume's argument involves several mistakes and fallacies. Our belief in testimony does not grow out of experience, although as the result of experience it is regulated. Nor does our belief in the uniformity of nature spring exclusively or ultimately from this source. On Hume's philosophy no reason can be assigned for expecting the course of nature to remain unaltered. Why should the future be, and the past have been, conformed to what we observe at present? We grant, however, that there is a rational presumption in favor of the uniformity of nature, and against the

Its fallacies.

---

[1] South's Sermon on The Certainty of our Saviour's Resurrection.

occurrence of a miracle. The very word "miracle," pointing to the wonder excited by such an event, implies a counter-expectation. But when Hume assumes that experience is uniform against the occurrence of miracles, he begs the question. The evidence for the unbroken uniformity of nature, as J. S. Mill has correctly stated, is diminished in force by whatever weight belongs to the evidence that certain miracles have taken place.[1] Hume separates a miracle from every conceivable object. He looks at it as a perfectly isolated occurrence—a bare marvel. His fundamental error consists in arguing the question on the tacit assumption of atheism. He ignores the existence of a cause adequate to work miracles, and, of course, the existence of any motive or occasion for them to be wrought. If the righteous God, whose existence and attributes are verified in Natural Theology, could be deemed as likely to subvert the laws which justify belief in human testimony, as—for example —to heal a man born blind, in order to furnish a sign and proof that salvation has been provided from spiritual darkness and sin, Hume's reasoning would be more plausible. In other words, he virtually takes it for granted that one miracle—a miracle for a purpose of deception—is as much to be expected as another miracle, wrought for a worthy and merciful end. All that Hume has made out,

[1] Mill's System of Logic, vol. ii., p. 185.

as Mill explains, is that no evidence can prove a miracle to an atheist, or to a deist who supposes himself able to prove that God would not interfere to produce the miraculous event in question. Mill adds truly "that natural religion is the necessary basis of revealed; that the proofs of Christianity presuppose the being and moral attributes of God; that it is the conformity of a religion to those attributes which determines whether credence ought be given to its external evidences."[1]

<small>J. S. Mill on Hume's argument.</small>

Professor Huxley, in his comments on Hume, objects to Hume's definition of a miracle as a violation of the laws of nature, "because all we know of the order of nature is derived from an observation of the course of events of which the so-called miracle is a part."[2] He admits that an event of this character is capable of being proved by testimony; but he appears to think that, if thus established, it would be an occurrence under the laws of nature, and would be referable to natural causes. This explanation, however, in many conceivable cases, would be irrational. If a man is known to be dead and is awakened to life at the command of another, the effect could not be referred to natural causes. If it could, a superhuman knowledge of natural causes would have to be as-

<small>Huxley's position.</small>

---

[1] Mill's System of Logic, vol. ii., p. 186.
[2] Huxley's Hume, p. 131.

cribed to him who gave the command, and this would involve miracle. The coincidence of the occurrence with the word or act of a person "proves design in the marvel, and makes it a miracle; and if that person professes to report a message or revelation from heaven, the coincidence again of the miracle with the professed message of God proves design on the part of God to warrant and authorize the message." That is to say, the occurrence of the marvel at the moment when the man is bidden to arise cannot be a *mere* coincidence.

<small>Miracle proves design.</small>

5. The question is sometimes asked, How can we be certain that an effect which exceeds the power of natural causes, does not spring from the agency of a superhuman evil being? There are certain miracles, such, in particular, as imply the exertion of creative power, which it appears unreasonable to attribute to any created being. But, apart from this consideration, there may be collateral proof—moral evidence— that shows the miracle to be the work of no evil being, and of no other being than God. It is to such evidence that, according to the Gospel narrative, Jesus appeals in answer to the allegation that his miracles were wrought by the help of evil spirits.[1]

<small>Can evil spirits work miracles?</small>

[1] Matt. xii. 25, 26; Mark xiii. 23, 24; Luke xi. 17, 18.

What is the distinctive office and place of miracles among the evidences of Revelation? In the first place, it is plain that Revelation, as distinguished from the manifestation of God in the course of nature and the ordinary doings of Providence, is in its very idea miraculous. It is a more direct disclosure of God than is elsewhere afforded. This fact of the presence and more immediate agency of God in connection with religious doctrine is signified to the senses by works of supernatural power. These works corroborate the evidence furnished by the doctrine itself, and by all the proofs of a moral nature that attend the promulgation of it. Miracles are aids to faith. They come in with decisive effect to convince those who are impressed by the moral evidence that they are not deceived, and that God is in reality speaking through men. According to the New Testament histories it was in this light that miracles were regarded by Jesus. Where there was no spiritual preparation, no dawning faith, he refused to perform miracles. He set the highest value upon the moral proofs.[1] Yet he considered the miracles to be of use in proving himself to be the messenger of God and to have power committed to him to forgive sin.[2]

<small>Proof from miracles and from doctrine.</small>

[1] John xiv. 11.
[2] Matt. ix. 6; Mark ii. 10; Luke ix. 24.

Thus it appears that while the doctrine proves the miracles the miracles prove the doctrine. They are two mutually supporting species of proof. They are both parts of one manifestation of God, neither of which is to be relied upon to the exclusion of the other, as if the other were of no value.

<small>Mutual support of doctrine and miracles.</small>

CHAPTER III.

HOW THE ANTECEDENT PRESUMPTION AGAINST THE OCCURRENCE OF MIRACLES IS SET ASIDE.

By a presumption is meant such a previous likelihood that a given statement is true or false as justly predisposes one to believe or to reject it. On the ground of some principle, or prior conviction, which is based on evidence, we bring to the consideration of a question a favorable or an adverse pre-judgment. This may have different degrees of strength, varying with the character of the evidence on which it rests. If we hear that one known to be a miser has made a large gift to the poor, or that one known to be a generous philanthropist has refused to relieve a worthy person who was in distress, there is a presumption in each case that the report is false. What gives rise to the presumption against the truth of the proposition that a miracle has occurred is the known fact of the uniformity of nature and the obvious benefit of such an arrangement. On the ground of this faith in an established course of nature, we feel justified in passing over, without credence, and even

Meaning of "presumption."

without inquiry, stories of miracles which are met with in historians whose records of ordinary occurrences we have no hesitation in believing. We give credit to what Tacitus relates about the wars of Vespasian, but when he tells the story of the healing of a blind man by that Emperor, we smile at the tale, or at most try to conjecture in what way the erroneous report had arisen. To set aside this presumption against the miraculous, it is requisite that we should discern the need of a Revelation and appreciate in some degree the intrinsic excellence of the Christian system. Then the way will be open to examine the evidence which shows that the miracles recorded in the New Testament were actually wrought.

"I deem it unnecessary to prove," says Paley, "that mankind stood in need of a revelation, because I have met with no serious person who thinks that, even under the Christian revelation, we have too much light, or any degree of persuasion which is superfluous." The anterior probability that a revelation will be given lies in the necessitous condition of man and the benevolent character of God.

Antecedent probability of revelation.

There is no interest of man so important as religion. It is vitally connected with his obligations and his destiny. In relation to this subject there are four principal sources of anxiety and distress. The first is the vagueness and uncertainty of man's

THE NEED OF REVELATION.

knowledge, under the light of nature, of God and divine things. The question is not what is theoretically *possible* to be ascertained on these themes, or what the extent of the native power of reason is, but rather what man, in his present condition and character, actually does discover or can be expected to discover.

The need of revelation. Four points:
1. The need of knowledge.

We find that there is neither absolute ignorance and a satisfied state of ignorance, nor is there such a vividness and certainty of conviction as give rest to the mind and furnish an adequate incentive to right conduct. Man "feels after God," gropes in the dark as for an object of which he knows something, but which he cannot find and grasp. We perceive that men oscillate between gross superstition and a dismal unbelief. On the question of the immortality of the soul there is a like uncertainty, a mixture of hope and doubt. This was the position of a man so virtuous and elevated as Socrates.

There is, besides, a sense of unworthiness which haunts the mind and often becomes an oppressive burden. There is a sense of guilt which reveals itself in the rites of the religions of the heathen nations. It is the consciousness of being unreconciled to the Power on whom we depend and to whom a more or less distinct feeling of responsibility prevails among mankind.

2. The guilt of sin.

Moreover, there is a feeling of discontent and

helplessness under the dominion which evil has acquired in the heart. There is a bondage of habit which often gives rise to an ineffectual struggle and to a craving for supernatural help. A heathen poet expresses the sense of this slavery, when he says: "I see and approve what is good; I do what is evil."

3. The bondage of sin.

> "Video meliora proboque;
> Deteriora sequor."—OVID.

Even Byron speaks of

> "This uneradicable taint of sin,
> This boundless upas, this all-blasting tree—"

In addition to these necessities of the soul, there is the need, under the sufferings of life, of sources of strength, such as the light of nature does not afford. Relief under afflictions, peace in sorrow, salvation from despondency, are wants which are deeply felt.

4. The burden of pain and sorrow.

We cannot dwell on these great facts respecting mankind. No one who interrogates his own conscience, and looks abroad on the world and over the field of history, can fail to be impressed by them.

While there is a great need of man to be supplied, a need which experience proves that he cannot himself supply through his own unaided powers, there are, likewise, indications in nature of the benevolence of God.

The benevolence of God.

This character is brought to light in the teachings of Natural Theology. Even heathen writers—for example, Plutarch—have written on the Delay of God in punishing the wicked, and have inferred His compassion and desire to save the unworthy.

The way in which Christianity meets the deep wants of human nature which have been briefly described, is one strong proof of its divine origin. It forms an important portion of the internal evidence of the truth of the Gospel, and of its being a revelation from God. But in this place, where we are only considering whether there is a probability that miracles will occur—such a probability as sets aside the contrary presumption—we can only call attention to features of the Christian system which everybody must acknowledge to exist.

Christianity meets the needs of man.

1. Christianity sets forth the main truths of natural religion in a clear and vivid form. The being of God, his moral and providential government, man's accountableness, the future life, are taught, and are taught so impressively that, as a matter of fact, multitudes of men have been persuaded of their truth, and have been moved to cast aside heathen superstitions, as well as skepticism and disbelief.

It sets forth the truths of natural religion.

2. Christianity does not hide or extenuate the evil which has been depicted above. It brings out

with emphasis the sin and guilt of men, and whatever is distressing in their lot, including their mortality. In short, Christianity recognizes the full extent of the malady and professes to grapple with it.

<small>It recognizes the malady.</small>

3. Christianity makes definite provisions to meet the great wants which have been specified, viz., the vagueness of our knowledge of God, the stings of conscience, the need of fresh incentives, and of spiritual aid from without, for the conflict with evil habit within the soul, and to lighten the burdens of sorrow and affliction.

<small>Remedies provided.</small>

Not only does Christianity undertake thus to bring men to a true knowledge of God and fellowship with Him, but history shows that, in innumerable instances, this result has been effected. Strength to bear the heaviest troubles has been gained, together with peace and the light of hope in the presence of death.

The moral precepts of Christianity are conformed to the dictates of conscience. These precepts, as far as they relate to our relations to one another, may be comprised under the heads of veracity, purity, kindness. Sincerity in speech and conduct, chastity in thought and behavior, benevolence, sympathy, charitableness in judgment and action, are the leading injunctions of the Gospel.

<small>The ethics of Christianity.</small>

The history of Christianity proves that the practice of these virtues is facilitated, and the conquest over the opposite vices is achieved, by means of the faith and hope of the Gospel. In other words, the religion of the Gospel, entering into the convictions and experience of the soul, is a most effective instrument of moral reform. The legitimate result of Christianity, it is not too much to say, is "a new creation" of spiritual and ethical character.

<small>Connection of faith and morals.</small>

These considerations are sufficient to neutralize the presumption against miracles in connection with Christianity and to place them on the same level, as regards proof, with matters of fact where no miracle is involved. For, if the miracles were subtracted, its distinctive character as a direct approach of God to man would be lost, an essential side of the evidence of its truth would vanish, and its practical efficacy would be to a great extent paralyzed. In judging of Christianity, it is desirable to remember, as Paley observes, that "the question lies between this religion and none; for, if the Christian religion be not credible, no one with whom we have to do will support the pretensions of any other"—certainly not the pretensions of any other to a supernatural origin and a miraculous attestation.

CHAPTER IV.

ADMITTED FACTS RESPECTING CHRISTIANITY.

Before proceeding further, it is well to remind the reader how much there is in Christianity that is not a subject of dispute. Let us glance at some of the admitted facts. Christianity originated in the short ministry of Jesus of Nazareth. This ministry was preceded by the preaching of John the Baptist, to whose preaching and the effect of it the Jewish historian, Josephus, refers.[1] Jesus selected and trained a small company of disciples, who, like himself, were of a humble rank in life. He taught not longer than about three years, from place to place, in Palestine. He was condemned by the Jewish Sanhedrim, and was put to death under Pontius Pilate, the Roman Procurator in Judea. The religion of the Jews, among whom he was born and grew up, was a pure form of monotheism. In it was involved an expectation of a universal divine kingdom, of which the "Messiah" was to be the head. Jesus professed to be the ex-

Its origin in the life of Jesus.

The Jewish religion.

[1] Antiq., xviii. v. 2.

pected Messiah, and on this account he was put to death. His teachings and his life had made a powerful impression. Soon after his death his chosen followers testified that he had risen, and manifested himself to them.

His alleged resurrection.

This alleged fact they proclaimed, and submitted to great sufferings, and some of them to a cruel death, on account of their faith and of the testimony which they gave respecting Jesus. A few years after the death of Jesus, Saul of Tarsus, who had been active in persecuting his followers, was converted to the Christian faith, and became an untiring and zealous preacher of it. In the face of persecution from Jews and heathen, and without the advantage of support from the learned, the rich, or any other of the influential classes, the new religion rapidly spread in the cities of the Roman Empire. The Roman historian, Tacitus, informs us that in the time of Nero, the Christians who were tortured and killed by that tyrant formed "a great multitude."[1] This was in 64 A.D. The younger Pliny, Proprætor in Pontus and Bithynia, under Trajan, reports to the Emperor, in 111 A.D., that the number of Christians in that region was so large that the heathen altars had been well-nigh deserted, and there had been no market for the sale of animals for sacrifice.[2] The Gospel continued to make

The conversion of Paul.

Rapid spread of the Gospel.

[1] Annal, xv. 44.   [2] Plin., Ep. 97.

progress, in spite of legal measures of persecution and the violence of mobs, and notwithstanding that more than one able Emperor engaged with energy in systematic efforts to exterminate its disciples. At length the Emperor himself, Constantine, became a convert, and (A.D. 313) proclaimed toleration. The old heathen religion of the Græco-Roman world disappeared. The new barbarian nations which subverted Rome embraced Christianity. It is the religion of the most powerful nations, whom it did so much to train and civilize. It is now professed by nearly a third of the world's population.

Christians were united together from the beginning in forms of organization. The Church grew up, and, under varying forms of polity and modes of worship, has perpetuated itself until the present day. Certain rites, such as Baptism, the Lord's Supper, and the observance of Sunday, have been continued since the days of the Apostles. Numberless productions — theological, devotional, or otherwise practical — have emanated from Christian teachers, or from other Christian disciples in successive ages.

The Church and its rites.

It is allowed that the influence of Christianity has not been superficial, but of a profound, transforming character upon the individual and upon society. It has deeply affected art, literature, and laws, the sentiments and conduct of mankind. Whatever evil has been

The influence of Christianity.

done in the name of the Christian religion, is due, as is generally conceded, not to that religion itself, but to the perversion and corruption of it. With the possible exception of a few eccentric individuals, it is universally judged that the influence of Christianity upon human nature and upon civilization is altogether elevating and wholesome.

These bare outlines may serve to remind the reader how grand a phenomenon Christianity is in the history of the world. The question which we have to consider is whether the New Testament histories give the true account of its origin. It will not do to dispose of this question by vague remarks on human credulity and the possibilities of self-deception and imposture. "To put aside the question of its origin"—of the origin of the Christian religion—"by telling us that mankind are easily deceived, is much the same as it would be to put aside the question about the origin of the Gulf Stream by telling us that water is an element very easily moved in different directions."[1]

The question must be met.

[1] Hopkins's Lectures on the Evidences of Christianity.

CHAPTER V.

PROOF OF THE SUPERNATURAL ORIGIN OF CHRISTIANITY FROM THE PORTRAITURE OF THE CHARACTER OF JESUS IN THE EVANGELISTS.

The character of Jesus as it is depicted in the Evangelists is one of unequalled excellence. This is universally admitted. It is not a character made up of negative virtues alone, where the sole merit <small>Combination of virtues.</small> is the absence of culpable traits. It has positive, strongly marked features. It combines piety, an absorbing love and loyalty to God, with philanthropy—a love to men without any alloy of selfishness, and too strong to be conquered by their injustice and ingratitude. It unites thus, in perfect harmony, the qualities of the saint and of the philanthropist. It blends holiness with compassion and gentleness. There is no compromise with evil, no consent to the least wrong-doing, even in a friend or follower. But with this purity there is a deep well of tenderness, a spirit of forgiveness which never fails. With the active virtues, with an intrepidity that quails before none, however high in station and public esteem, there are connected the

THE CHARACTER OF JESUS. 33

passive virtues of patience, forbearance, meekness. The world beholds in Jesus its ideal of goodness.[1]

Now, there are conclusive reasons for affirming that this character is not the product of the imagination of the Evangelists. It is an *original* character, and one which those who describe it could never have invented. In the first place, it stands out in bold relief and in obvious contrast with the imperfections of those to whom we owe the portrait of it. With no model in actual life to follow, how could the fishermen of Galilee put on the canvas this figure—the central figure in the world's history? In the second place, it is not a character which is formally delineated. It is not set forth in a string of epithets, or abstract statements, or by vague, indiscriminate laudation. The impression which we gain of the character of Jesus is from a large collection of incidents and of sayings recorded in the Gospels. Our idea of him is the effect of a great variety of

<small>The portraiture of Jesus not contrived.</small>

[1] Speculative opinions not accordant with the faith of the Church have not availed to prevent candid minds from clearly discerning this fact. "It was reserved for Christianity to present to the world an ideal character, which through all the changes of eighteen centuries has inspired the hearts of men with an impassioned love, has shown itself capable of acting on all nations, ages, temperaments, and conditions, has been not only the highest pattern of virtue but the strongest incentive to its practice, and has exercised so deep an influence that it may be truly said that the simple record of three short years of active life has done more to regenerate and soften mankind than all the disquisitions of philosophers and all the exhortations of moralists."—Lecky's History of European Morals, vol. ii., p. 9.

facts. To the production of such an effect by such means, the writers, had they drawn upon their own imagination, or that of others, would have been manifestly incompetent. Finally, the character of Jesus, as portrayed in the Gospels, has an unmistakable air of reality.

We may go forward with safety a step farther. Jesus, as we become acquainted with him in the Gospel narratives, which are to this extent self-verifying, was literally a sinless person. We have here a character of immaculate purity. This, to be sure, is a point which cannot be *demonstrated*, since no one can discern the motives of action; but it can be established beyond reasonable doubt. In all that is recorded of him, there is no evidence of moral fault. There is nothing that he did or said which can justly be made a ground of reproach. It is incredible that the Evangelists, even on the supposition of a plan on their part to make him out to be better than he was, could have selected their materials—putting in this, and leaving out that—in such a way as to accomplish the purpose. The task would have been too great for their powers. It would imply not only a perfect ideal in their minds, but, also, an impossible skill in realizing it in a narrative form.

Moreover, while Jesus was obviously holy beyond all example, and had the clearest, most penetrating discernment of moral evil, and

Perfection of the character of Jesus.

No self-reproach.

while he condemned even the least wrong in the inmost thoughts and intents of the soul, there is not a trace of self-reproach on his part. Had he anywhere, even in his prayers to God, implied that he was guilty of fault, some record of his self-accusation would have been left. It would have found its way into the traditions concerning him. When his cause was prostrate, and nothing but an ignominious death awaited him, in the hours of anguish some expression implying penitence would have escaped him. Not only is there no trace of such a feeling on his part, but it will scarcely be denied that he made on his followers, who were intimately associated with him, the impression that he was absolutely free from moral fault.

Those who are convinced that Jesus was without sin may find in the fact a cogent argument for the supernatural origin of Christianity. In the first place, there is no reason to think that any other faultless and perfect character has ever existed among men. Jesus is thus an exception to a universal fact respecting the race. To account for this exception, to explain this one instance of spotless purity, it is reasonable to assume an extraordinary relation to God on his part—to assume something that is equivalent to a miracle. In the second place, his sinlessness gives credibility to his testimony respecting himself. That he claimed to be the Son of God, the Messiah,

The perfection of Jesus a miraculous fact.

is beyond all dispute. On this charge he was crucified. It will not be questioned that the position which he claimed, and persisted in claiming, was of an exceptional and exalted kind. It will not be questioned that he considered himself the spiritual guide and deliverer of mankind. To acquit him of an unheard-of arrogance and self-deception we must give credit to his judgment and testimony concerning himself. If we discredit this judgment and testimony we must conclude that perfect moral purity, and humility withal, are consistent with a self-exaltation alike baseless and really without a parallel in the extent to which it was carried. We must ascribe to him an enormous self-delusion. We must conclude of the only pure and perfect one that the light that was in him was "darkness."

The safeguard against self-deception.

CHAPTER VI.

PROOF OF THE MIRACLES FROM PECULIAR FEATURES OF THE GOSPEL NARRATIVES.

No one doubts that the Gospels contain a great deal that is true about the life and teaching of Christ. These books are the almost exclusive source from which the world derives its knowledge of what he did and suffered and of what he said. Such writers as Strauss and Rénan, who disbelieve in the miracles, construct biographies of Jesus out of the materials furnished them in the Gospels.

Now, before inquiring into the date and authorship of these four histories, we can find in what all candid students must concede to be historically true in them, convincing proof that miracles were wrought by Jesus.

1. On different occasions Jesus is said to have told those whom he miraculously healed not to make it publicly known.[1] He wished to avoid a public excitement having little or no kinship with moral and spiritual

The prohibitions to report miracles.

---

[1] Matt. ix. 30, xii. 16, xvii. 9; Mark iii. 12, v. 43; Luke v. 14, viii. 56, etc.

feeling. Sometimes he had to retire to solitary places to avoid the multitude. No one can reasonably question that these injunctions not to report miracles were uttered by him. There is no motive that could account for the invention of them, especially since it is added that they were disregarded.

2. Cautions, which are plainly authentic, against an excessive esteem of miracles, are said to have been uttered by Jesus.[1] No one who made up stories of miracles would connect with his accounts a disparagement of them, or anything that looked like it. The imaginative, wonder-loving spirit, which prompts to the invention of fictitious miracles, always magnifies their importance. The disciples, when they rejoiced that they had been able to deliver demoniacs, were told not to rejoice that the spirits were subject to them, but rather to rejoice that they could look forward to an abode in heaven.[2]

Miracles not overvalued.

3. There are sayings of Christ which are evidently genuine, but which are inseparable from the miracles with which they are connected in the record. Thus, John the Baptist, when he was in prison, sent two of his disciples to Jesus to inquire if he were in truth the Messiah or only a forerunner.[3] This inquiry implies a momentary doubt in the mind of John, owing, it is to be

Teaching and miracles linked together.

---

[1] John iv. 48, xiv. 11; Matt. xvi. 3; Luke x. 17.   [2] Luke x. 20
[3] Matt. xi. 4; Luke xvii. 22.

presumed, to the fact that no grand demonstration of the power of Christ had been made, no visible establishment of a kingdom. Perhaps the gloom of a prison may have had its influence in exciting this transient doubt. But such a doubt in the mind of the prophet, of him whose testimony to Jesus was counted of so much value, no disciple of Jesus would have wished to occur. No one would think of falsely attributing it to John. The messengers were directed to go back to John and to tell him what they had seen and heard: "The blind receive their sight, and the lame walk; the lepers are cleansed, and the deaf hear; the dead are raised up, and the poor have the Gospel preached to them." This answer of Jesus is part and parcel of the incident. It is inseparable from the question. And the incident proves that Jesus was engaged in working the miracles of which mention is made.

Among the controversies of Jesus with over-rigid observers of the sabbath, there is one in which he is said to have put the question: "Which of you shall have an ass or an ox fallen into a pit, and will not straightway pull him out on the sabbath day?"[1] These words are in a style characteristic of Jesus. Few, if any, doubt that he uttered them. Now, Luke says that the occasion of the question was a reproach from the Pharisees for healing a man of the dropsy. The words obviously imply that it was a case where

[1] Luke xiv. 5.

some one who was in extreme danger had been rescued. How can it be doubted that Jesus had really, as the Evangelist relates, healed a man of a dangerous disease on the sabbath day?

Other similar instances might be adduced. One who studies the Gospels will see that the teachings of Jesus presuppose the miracles which are recorded in conjunction with his reported words having reference to them.

The Evangelists ascribe to Jesus no miracles prior to his baptism. This is one striking difference between them and the apocryphal Gospels. If the record of miracles by the Evangelists is not true, if they are creations of fancy or invention, why do they not commence earlier? Why are not miracles ascribed to Jesus before he reached the age of thirty? Why is this long period left a blank?

<small>No miracles prior to the baptism of Jesus.</small>

Moreover, no miracles are attributed to John the Baptist, notwithstanding that so much value is attached in the Gospels to his testimony to Jesus. If there had been a disposition to make up stories of miracles that did not occur, why is not John credited with works of a like nature?

<small>No miracles ascribed to the Baptist.</small>

CHAPTER VII.

PROOF OF THE RESURRECTION OF JESUS FROM STATEMENTS BY THE APOSTLE PAUL.

There are four Epistles which no competent scholar doubts that the Apostle Paul wrote. The most noted schools of modern skeptics have with one accord accepted them as genuine. They are the two Epistles to the Corinthians, and the Epistles to the Romans and Galatians. In his first Epistle to the Corinthians, Paul refers to the proofs of the resurrection of Jesus. In this important passage we are told what he had learned from the other Apostles on this subject. In the Epistle to the Galatians he speaks of his intercourse with them on different occasions. Three years after his conversion, he had spent a fortnight with Peter at Jerusalem (Gal. i. 18). At that time he had met James, the Lord's brother. Later (A.D. 52), he met Peter, James, and John, and conferred with them on the Gospel (Gal. ii. 1–10). He had enjoyed ample opportunities to ascertain what the Apostles had to say about the resurrection of Jesus; that he would avail himself of these

The acquaintance of Paul with the other Apostles.

opportunities we might be certain beforehand; but that he did so, what he tells us on the subject proves.

<small>What he had learned from them.</small> Writing to the Corinthians, he sets down distinctly what he had previously declared to them respecting the Saviour's reappearance from the dead.[1] On the third day after his burial, Jesus appeared to Peter. Afterwards he appeared to the twelve; then to above five hundred brethren assembled together; then to James; then to all the Apostles. Last of all, he had manifested himself alive to Paul himself at the time of his conversion; for to this event he undoubtedly refers. Even without the records of the Evangelists, it is safe to conclude, from these statements in the Epistle to the Corinthians, that the Apostles, from the third day after the death of Jesus, testified, substantially as related by Paul, to his resurrection. We have, therefore, the testimony of the Apostles to this cardinal fact in the Gospel history, and that testimony is entitled to credit.

It is said, by way of objection, that the alleged manifestation of Jesus to Paul was in a vision, and <small>Paul saw Jesus.</small> that this may have been unreal. But, first, Paul distinguishes the first revelation of Jesus to him, when he saw Jesus, from subsequent visions and revelations (2 Cor. xii. 1; 1 Cor. ii. 10). "*Last of all,*" he says, enumerating the

[1] 1 Cor. xv. 1-9.

appearances of the risen Jesus, "he appeared to me also." Whether by "all" is here meant all interviews with the risen Jesus, or all of the Apostles, the inference following from the statement is the same. Paul's sight of Jesus at his conversion was the last of the series of his bodily manifestations, as distinguished from apocalyptic visions. Secondly, even if there were any reason to regard these last as unreal, his first perception of Christ could not be accounted for in this way. We shall show hereafter that Paul's mind was not in such a state as to permit us to ascribe that first revelation to him to the effect of hallucination. We shall find him assuring us that he had not felt the least doubt as to the rectitude of the course that he was pursuing in his warfare on the disciples. He had not the slightest misgivings on the subject. The expression: "It is hard for thee to kick against the pricks," is a proverb denoting the futility of the attempt to withstand the progress of Christ's cause. It has no reference to inward feelings of Paul, as if he were disturbed by doubt and a divided mind. He verily thought that he was doing God service.

Whatever the nature of the alleged manifestation of Jesus to Paul was, there is no reason to interpret him as saying that the appearances of Jesus to the other Apostles were of the same kind as to him. If we turn to the Gospels, we find accounts of interviews of the risen Jesus with his followers, which, to say the least, are the earliest and the only traditions that were handed down in the early Church. This can be safely affirmed before we examine the question of the authorship of the Gospels. There is certainly, even at this stage of our discussion, no reason to doubt that these accounts in the Gospels embody the statements which the Apostles made to their converts. At all events, Paul's letter to the Corinthians establishes the point that they testified to the interviews which he there enumerates.

Were the Apostles deceived? Were these manifestations to them (and to the five hundred) a delusion of their own minds? Hallucination is a disorder of the senses, or of the brain, which leads one to see or to hear what has no reality outside of the nervous organism. This explanation of the appearances of Jesus to the Disciples after his death, is excluded for several reasons that are decisive. There is no probability that they were looking for any such reappearance of Christ. There is no reason to distrust, but good reasons for believing, the statements of the Evangelists that the disciples, although they did not disperse, or forsake Jerusalem, were affected with sorrow and fear. This would be natural on finding themselves bereaved of their Master, and their hopes connected with him crushed by an event so appalling as his crucifixion. There was, then, no

The hallucination theory.

preparation of mind for such a delusion as the hallucination theory implies. Then, the fact that so many persons, in companies, on different occasions, were persuaded, without a shadow of doubt, that Christ was with them, and that they saw him, renders such an hypothesis the more improbable. When the authenticity of the Gospels shall have been established, the circumstances related by them —for example, the doubts of Thomas and the way they were overcome—will be seen absolutely to preclude the theory in question. But, besides these considerations, the idea of hallucination is shut out by one remarkable peculiarity of the alleged manifestations of the risen Jesus. They took place, as Paul's testimony shows, at intervals, and in a definite number. They began at a certain time—on the third day; and they ended after a brief period. Had the followers of Jesus been in that state of mind out of which the illusions of hallucination might arise, and if this had been the source of what they thought to be actual reappearances of Jesus, these manifestations would have been much more numerous. They would not have begun and ended at these definite points. They would not have suddenly ceased. They would have continued and multiplied as time went on, and as the courage and enthusiasm of the flock increased. This would surely have been the case, according to the ordinary law of the working of this sort of mental delusion.

The conclusion is justified that the testimony of the Apostles, to which they adhered at the cost of every earthly comfort and of life itself—for there is no doubt that they steadfastly endured these penalties—ought to be believed.

CHAPTER VIII.

THE GENUINENESS OF THE GOSPELS.

The evidence of the genuineness of the Gospels is the same in kind as the evidence which satisfies us of the genuineness of the History of the Jews (ascribed to Josephus), of Livy's History of Rome, and of other writings, whether ancient or modern. The early reception of writings as genuine by those who had the means of knowing, early traditions respecting them which are not justly liable to suspicion, references to them, or quotations from them, at a time when, if they were spurious, this fact could not have been concealed, internal marks in the works themselves indicative of their authorship or date of composition—these are among the proofs on which we rely in determining the question of the origin of literary works.

Nature of the proofs.

In glancing at the evidence on this subject, in the present case, we will first take our stand in the closing part of the second century. It is allowed on all hands that the four Gospels of the canon were at that time the sole and universally recognized authorities concerning the life of Jesus, in all the churches in the different regions of the Roman Empire. From this starting-point we will travel backward to the immediate neighborhood of the Apostolic age.

One of the most famous and influential men in the Church in the last quarter of the second century was Irenæus, who became bishop of Lyons, in Gaul, A.D. 177. Not far from A.D. 180 he wrote an elaborate work against the heresies which had sprung up in that century. In the course of this work he has occasion to speak of the Four Gospels as received by all the churches, and received exclusively. He does not speak of this fact as anything new, or as if he had ever heard of anything different, or as if there could be any reasonable doubt that this exclusive rank belonged to the Four. According to Irenæus, one might as well think of more or less than four quarters of the earth, of more or less than the four winds. He tells us, moreover, in detail,[1] that Matthew published "a written Gospel among the Hebrews in their own language," that after the death of Peter and Paul, "Mark, Peter's disciple and interpreter, did himself also publish unto us in writing the things which were preached by Peter"; that "Luke, too, the attendant of Paul, set down in a book the Gospel preached by him"; that "afterwards John, the disciple of the Lord, who also leaned on his breast—he again put forth his Gospel while he abode

[1] Adv. Haer., III., i., 1.

THE GENUINENESS OF THE GOSPELS. 49

in Ephesus in Asia." Elsewhere,[1] Irenæus informs us that John lived to an advanced age, and did not die until after the accession of Trajan (A.D. 98).

Of the integrity of Irenæus there is no question. We have only to ascertain what means he had of acquainting himself with the past. He was born in Asia Minor, and spent the early part of his life in the East. He well remembered Polycarp, the martyr, Bishop of Smyrna, who was an acquaintance and disciple of the Apostle John himself.[2] Polycarp was put to death A.D. 155. How long it was before his death that Irenæus had intercourse with him we are not told, but it was when Irenæus himself was young. He was probably born between A.D. 120 and A.D. 130. Besides the memorable fact of his acquaintance with Polycarp, Irenæus was familiar with many Christian disciples who were old when he was a youth. Pothinus, whose colleague he was for a while at Lyons, before he succeeded him as bishop, lived to the age of ninety years. He died A.D. 177. Irenæus had conferred with "elders"—that is, venerated leaders in the Church of an earlier time, who had been pupils of men whom the Apostles had instructed, and some of whom had sat at the feet of the Apostles themselves.[3]

<small>Value of the testimony of Irenæus.</small>

[1] Adv. Haer., II., xxii., 5.
[2] Adv. Haer., III., iii., 4; Epist. ad Flor.
[3] Adv. Haer., II., xxii., 5; III., i., 1; III., iii., 4; V., xxx., 1; IV., xxxii., 1; cf. Eusebius, Hist. Eccl., III., 23; IV., 14; V., 8.

A like testimony to the universal exclusive reception of the Four Gospels, as the authorities handed down in the churches, is given by other distinguished church teachers, contemporaries of Irenæus. We hear substantially the same thing from Clement, a renowned theological teacher at Alexandria, and from Tertullian, who was a leading presbyter in North Africa. Clement was born not later than A.D. 160. Referring to a statement in an apocryphal Gospel, he remarks that it is not found "in the four Gospels which have been handed down to us."[1] Clement was a man of learning who had, moreover, travelled extensively. The four Gospels, Tertullian asserts, have existed from "the very beginning," and "are coeval with the churches themselves."[2] His appeal is to the testimony of churches which the Apostles themselves founded.

We now go back to the generation prior to Irenæus. Here we have the testimony of Justin Martyr. Justin was put to death for being a Christian, under Marcus Aurelius, probably A.D. 166. At the time of the Jewish rebellion of Bar-cochba (A.D. 134–136), he had already pursued extensive studies in various schools of philosophy, and had been converted to the Christian faith. He was born, it is believed, at the close of the first century. His birthplace was the Roman

---

[1] Strom., III., 553 (ed. Potter).   [2] Adv. Marcion, IV., 5.

colony of Flavia Neapolis, near the ancient Sichem, in Samaria; but his family was Greek. He sojourned for a time at Ephesus. He had a wide acquaintance with Christians, and with their churches in many places. Three of his writings are extant — two "Apologies," or Defences of Christianity, and the Dialogue with Trypho, a Jew. The first of his Apologies was addressed to Antoninus Pius, about 148; the second followed not long after the first. The sources from which Justin draws his accounts of the life and teachings of Jesus he styles *Memoirs,* or *Memoirs of the Apostles.* Writing for disbelievers outside of the Church, he has no occasion to refer to the authors of them by name. But he describes them as written by Apostles and their companions. This he does in connection with a passage that is found in Luke.[1] This description answers to the Four, two of whom bear the names of Apostles, and the other two were ascribed to attendants of Apostles. In one place he refers to an incident respecting Peter, which he professes to derive from "his Gospel."[2] The incident is found in Mark, which, as we know from other sources, was not unfrequently called Peter's Gospel. Another reading of the text in Justin, however, would make the reference to be, as in other places, to the Memoirs of "the Apostles." He calls the Memoirs, in one

[1] Dial. c. 103.   [2] Dial., c. 108.

place, "Gospels."[1] Twice he refers to "the Gospel,"[2] a title given in other authors to the Four collectively. Justin says that the Memoirs were in public use. They were read on Sunday in the religious services of Christians, "in city and country."[3] What were these "Memoirs"? They must have been the same as those described by Irenæus. If not, it must be assumed that after Irenæus had grown up to manhood, the authoritative Gospels in use in the Churches were superseded by others, or else that new Gospels, not previously acknowledged, took their place by the side of such as had previously been accepted. But how could so important changes take place, and Irenæus know nothing of them?

But the references to the contents of the Memoirs in Justin are very numerous. When they are brought together they make up a pretty full account of the events in the life of Jesus, and of his sayings. They correspond to the statements of the canonical Evangelists. A large part of the matter accords with what we find in Matthew and Luke; a small portion of it is found in Mark alone; and there are not wanting striking correspondences to passages occurring exclusively in John. It is true that the quotations are not verbally accurate. For Justin's purpose there was no occasion that they

Correspondence of the quotations to the Gospels of the Canon.

[1] Apol., I, c. 66.   [2] Dial., cc. 10, 100.   [3] Apol., I. 67

should be. But his quotations from the Gospels are not more free, as to their form, than are his references to Old Testament passages. He does not even think it necessary to cite a passage the second time in the same words. His verbal inaccuracy in quoting John (John iii. 3–5) was a natural one, and has been shown to be just the same as in a citation of the passage in so late a writer as the celebrated English divine, Jeremy Taylor.[1] Justin's references to events or sayings in the Gospel history, which have not substantial parallels in the Gospels of the Canon, are few and insignificant, and can be accounted for without supposing them to have been derived from other written sources. They embrace not more than two sayings of Jesus, both of which are found in other writers who yet own no authoritative Gospels but the four of the Canon.

An additional proof that Justin's Gospels were the four of the Canon is the fact that Tatian, who was a pupil of Justin, combined these four in a simple narrative, called *Diatessaron*, or the Gospel of the Four. It began with the opening passage of John's Gospel.

Tatian's harmony.

---

[1] Justin's words are: "For, indeed, Christ also said 'except ye be born again, ye shall not enter into the kingdom of heaven.' And that it is impossible for those who are once born to enter into their mothers' womb is plain to all." Not alone by the correspondence of passages in Justin with particular verses in John, is his use of this Gospel made evident. His teaching in respect to the Logos or Word must have been derived from a source recognized as authoritative; and no such source is known, unless it was the Fourth Gospel.

The Christian literature prior to the middle of the second century is scanty in amount, and fragmentary. It consists for the most part of letters, written for purposes of edification. Statements coincident with passages in the Gospels occur, but they are usually interwoven in the text, either without any express notice that they are quoted, or with an indefinite mention of them as being a part of authoritative Christian teaching. It is not always possible to tell with certainty whether such passages were taken from the oral tradition at the basis of the first three Gospels, or from these writings themselves. But we meet in the Apostolic Fathers, the writers of the sub-apostolic age, numerous echoes of the narratives which make up the contents of the four canonical Gospels.

Character of the earliest literature.

Polycarp. A few instances may be given of this character. Polycarp, in his Epistle to the Philippians,[1] has the words: "According as the Lord said, 'the spirit indeed is willing, but the flesh is weak.'" The quotation corresponds exactly to Matt. vi. 13, and was probably derived from this Gospel. In the same chapter, Polycarp says: "For every one who shall not confess that Jesus Christ is come in the flesh, is antichrist." This statement was taken from 1 John iv. 2–4, unless indeed it was remembered by Polycarp as having been uttered by his apostolic teacher. Without doubt, the Gospel

[1] C. vii.

of John and the first Epistle are from the same hand. The Epistle erroneously ascribed to Barnabas was written not later than A.D. 120. It contains several passages which it is most natural to refer to the Gospel of Matthew as their source. This appears almost certain respecting the passage, "He came not to call the righteous but sinners."[1] In another place it is said: "Let us take heed lest so be that we be found, as it is written, 'Many called, but few chosen.'"[2] The words quoted are identical with Matt. xx. 16, or xxii. 14. The preface—"it is written"—was the common prefix to citations from sacred Scripture. If it have this meaning here, the Gospel is placed on a level with the books of the Old Testament.

Epistle of Barnabas.

A very ancient document, called "The Teaching of the Twelve Apostles," was first published in 1883, a few years after its discovery in a library in Constantinople. It is held by some scholars to be older than the Epistle of Barnabas (A.D. 120), and even to be as early as the last years of the first century. If not so old as Barnabas, we are forbidden by internal marks from placing it later than A.D. 140. It is a kind of Church manual of instruction, characterized by a strong infusion of Jewish Christian peculiarities. This book contains passages which imply a use of the Gospels of Matthew and of Luke. In one place[3] it

Teaching of the XII. Apostles.

[1] C. v. 9; cf. Matt. ix. 13. [2] C. iv. 9. [3] C. xv.

says: "But your prayers and your alms and all your deeds so do ye, as ye have it in the Gospel of our Lord." The same word—the Greek for "Gospel"—occurs in three other places in the book. It is probable that the term denotes a written record. It is the name given in Origen and other early writers to the Four Gospels, taken collectively, or regarded as one body. As used in the Teaching, it may have the same meaning; or it may possibly designate a combination, or harmony, of Matthew and Luke, which was in the author's hands. The writings which are thus tacitly recognized in the Teaching must have been received as authorities in the churches for which it was written, and in which it was used. Besides the distinct traces of the use of these Gospels, the three Eucharistic prayers[1] contain words and phrases peculiar to John's Gospel. From this source it is natural to conclude that they were drawn.

The antiquity of the Gospels is proved by the ancient versions that were made. The Peshito, the Bible of the Syrian churches, originated, in all probability within the limits of the second century. Its origin is placed by the most competent scholars in the first half of that century. The Old Latin version was in current use when Tertullian wrote. It must have been made earlier than A.D. 170; how much earlier we cannot determine.

The ancient versions.

[1] Cc. ix. and x.

From a contemporary of Justin, but older than he—Papias, Bishop of Hierapolis, in Phrygia—we have definite accounts relative to the composition of the Gospels of Matthew and Mark. Papias was a contemporary of Polycarp (who was born A.D. 69 and died, as we have said, in 155). Papias was diligent in gathering information from those who had been conversant with the Apostles, and he appears to have conferred personally with two of the immediate disciples of Jesus, John, the Elder (as he is called), and Aristion. He was thought by Irenæus to have been acquainted with John, the Apostle, but this is doubted by the ancient church historian, Eusebius. Papias wrote a book entitled, "Exposition of the Oracles of the Lord." In this work, he says of John, the Elder, or Presbyter, in a passage quoted by Eusebius:

Testimony of Papias.

"And the Elder said this: "Mark, having become the interpreter of Peter, wrote down accurately what he remembered, not, however, recording in order what was either said or done by Christ. For neither did he hear the Lord nor follow him, but afterwards, as I have said, attended Peter," etc.

"Such," adds Eusebius, "is the relation in Papias concerning Mark. But concerning Matthew this is said: 'So then Matthew wrote the oracles in the Hebrew language, and everyone interpreted them as he was able.'"[1]

[1] Euseb., Hist. Eccl., iv., 30.

The language of Papias implies that the necessity of translating the Hebrew or Aramaic original of Matthew no longer existed. That is to say, Matthew in the Greek was in his hands. Some scholars are of opinion that the word for "oracles" in the foregoing extracts from Papias, should be rendered "discourses" or "sayings," and that the work which Matthew wrote in Aramaic consisted mostly of discourses of Jesus. To these, it is supposed, the narrative parts of the book were added, in connection with its translation into Greek. Whatever expansion the writing of Matthew may have received after it was first composed, the work was so far recognized as his production that it continued to bear his name. That it existed in its present form as early as the capture of Jerusalem by Titus (A. D. 70) will be proved hereafter from internal evidence. If any portion of the book had another author than Matthew, that author was a contemporary disciple of sufficient authority to secure an undisputed acceptance of what was thus connected with the Apostle's composition. This editor of Matthew would stand thus on a level with Mark and Luke.

A striking proof of the genuineness of the canonical Gospels is the use made of them by heretical leaders, by whom they are dealt with as having authority in the churches. From these Gospels they endeavor to draw support for their eccentric opinions. In behalf of the third

Marcion.

Gospel there is evidence of a peculiar character from the treatment of it by Marcion, the founder of a sect bearing his name. Marcion was an active and formidable heresiarch when Justin wrote his first Apology (A.D. 148). He was born in Pontus, in Asia Minor; he knew Polycarp; and he was in Rome as early as about A.D. 140. Owing to his one-sided zeal for Paul's doctrine, as he incorrectly understood it, he refused to acknowledge the other Apostles as authorized guides, and made up a Canon, or collection of Scriptures, out of Paul's Epistles, and the Gospel of Luke — striking out of Luke, however, passages which recognized the authority of the Old Testament law. The Gospel used by Marcion is demonstrated, and is now generally conceded, to have been a mutilated Luke. This mutilation of the third Gospel, in order to promote a sectarian purpose, and the whole proceeding of Marcion in the matter, make it clear that Luke's Gospel, as we have it, was at the time generally received in the churches. Marcion selected this Gospel for the reason that Luke was acknowledged to have been a disciple of Paul. It is a just inference that the canonical Gospel was an authoritative document in the churches when a considerable number of the younger contemporaries of the Apostles were still living.

Within the first three Gospels themselves there are distinct evidences of their early date, and whatever proves their early date, proves likewise their genuineness; since, in the lifetime of the Apostles, and under their eyes, forged compositions, had anybody wished or dared to frame them, could not have secured acceptance among those whom the Apostles guided and taught. The most convincing of these internal proofs is in the predictive passages respecting the destruction of Jerusalem and the Parousia, or Second Advent, of Christ. The first impression made by these passages in Matthew is that there was no time to intervene between the two events, and the impression made by the corresponding passages in Mark and in Luke is that the interval is to be brief. It is not requisite here to attempt to explain the passages in question, or to account for the peculiarity to which we allude. Whatever explanation is adopted, it remains evident that, had the Gospels been written at a later day, the association of the destruction of Jerusalem with the last Judgment, in the manner and form in which they appear to be connected by the Evangelists, especially in Matthew, would not exist. There would surely have been some explanation, some caution against so natural an inference, some indication that the two events were not to stand in so close juxtaposition. Whoever will candidly examine the passages referred to, will be persuaded that the first three Gospels were written before the generation that

Internal proof of the early date of the first three Gospels.

listened to Jesus had passed off the stage. Matthew was composed before Jerusalem was taken by Titus. In any revision of this Gospel later than this catastrophe, these perplexing passages would not have been left unexplained. Mark must likewise have preceded the capture of the city and the destruction of the temple; and Luke must have been written, if not before, within a short time after these momentous occurrences.

The first three Gospels—and the same will be found to be true of the fourth—abound in allusions Local references. to places, local customs, characteristic ideas and feelings, such as no counterfeiter, writing at a later day, could have wrought into the narratives. They are introduced without design. They are such as only contemporaries familiar with Palestine and the ways of the people could have been conversant with. Very rarely there may occur a reference of this sort which it is difficult to verify; but this is true of the best accredited ancient writers who have left us accounts of their own times. The atmosphere of the Gospels is that of Galilee and Judea in the days of the Apostles.

The third Gospel and the book of Acts were ascribed without dispute, in the ancient Internal proof of the genuineness of Luke. Church, to Luke, a companion of Paul —the same Luke who is referred to by the Apostle.[1] Both works are undeniably by the same

---

[1] Col. iv. 16; 2 Tim. iv. 11.

author. This is manifest from the style. The book of Acts refers to "the former treatise," which was also addressed to the same Theophilus to whom the Acts is inscribed.[1] The author of the third Gospel professes to have derived his information from careful inquiries made of immediate witnesses and participants in the events related.[2] He had learned the facts orally, or, it might be, in part from writings. His avowed purpose was to present an accurate, consecutive narrative. There is no reason for questioning the fact that this statement was made by the author of the Gospel, or for doubting its truth. That the author was really at times a companion of Paul is established by a peculiar, convincing piece of evidence. The narrative in Acts moves on as we should expect of a historian who has gathered his information from others, until he arrives at Troas.[3] Then there is a sudden transition to the first person plural—"immediately we endeavored to go into Macedonia." The use of the pronoun, implying the author's personal association with Paul, goes on until the Apostle reaches Philippi. Then it is dropped during the rest of the Apostle's second missionary journey. But he joins Paul again, it would appear, at Philippi,[4] and continues in his company all the way to Rome. The graphic description of the voyage and shipwreck

Its author an attendant of Paul.

---

[1] Acts i. 1; Luke i. 4. [2] Luke i. 3.
[3] Acts xvi. 10. [4] Acts xx. 5.

makes it almost impossible to doubt that it was written by one who saw what he relates. There is no reasonable explanation of this use of the pronoun "we" in these parts of the book except that the author of the Acts (and thus the author of the third Gospel) accompanied Paul for a time on his journey. The style of the "we" passages is in complete accord with that of the rest of the book. This of itself excludes the idea that they are quoted from a document not written by the author. We cannot attribute to him a purpose to deceive the reader on this point. Had he been capable of such a fraudulent intent he would have taken pains to make his pretended relation to Paul more conspicuous. He would not have left it to be detected and inferred by none but observing readers. This is not at all the manner of the framers of pseudonymous writings.

It has been alleged that the representation of the relation of Paul to the other leading Apostles, which
<small>Agreement of Acts with the statements of Paul.</small> is given in the Acts, and of Paul's teaching to theirs, is not consistent with what we learn from his Epistles. This charge applies especially to Acts xv., and to the account there of the conference at Jerusalem. The allegation is that there was hostility to Paul and his doctrine, on the part of Peter. This objection would imply that the author of the Acts, whoever he may have been, was a later writer and a deliberate deceiver. It is overthrown completely by Paul's own un-

equivocal statement that the other Apostles—Peter, James, and John—"added nothing" to him; that is, had nothing to add, by way of amendment, to his doctrine—and by his distinct assertion that they gave to him "the right hand of fellowship."[1] This disproves the notion that Peter was a judaizer. That there was a public conference is not excluded, but rather implied in Paul's language.[2] That the results of it were substantially as related in the Acts, admits of no reasonable doubt. James, and those of like mind with him, would not have been content with a less measure of accommodation to Jewish feeling, from the side of the Gentile converts. That they *were* content is established by Paul's testimony in the Galatians.

The fourth Gospel is distinguished by marked characteristics from the other three. It has a more full account of the labors of Jesus in Judea.

The fourth Gospel and the first three. According to the fourth Gospel his ministry extended over more than three years; whereas from the first three—looked at apart from the light thrown on them by the fourth—we should infer that it was limited to about one year. The style of the discourses in John differs from that of most of the sayings of Jesus recorded in the other Evangelists. But these differences do not amount to an inconsistency. As to the labors of Jesus in Judea, and the duration of his ministry, we find in

[1] Gal. ii. 6, 9.   [2] Gal. ii. 2.

THE GENUINENESS OF THE GOSPELS.

the other Gospels incidental corroboration of the statements in John.[1] We find in them, also, occasional utterances of Jesus in the same vein as that of the discourses in the fourth Gospel.[2] The language ascribed to Jesus, as far as it is like that of the Evangelist himself, and of other persons who appear in his narrative, may be accounted for naturally, if we suppose that John had assimilated the thoughts of his master, and presents them, in part, in a condensed form and in language of his own.

Peculiarities of the fourth Gospel prove its genuineness. These peculiarities of the fourth Gospel are really an argument for its genuineness, for they are such as no forger, no one falsely assuming to be an Apostle, would have ventured to impart to his composition. He would rather have sought to imitate, as far as he could, the earlier, acknowledged, and well-known Gospels. Having these striking peculiarities, it would have been suspected and rejected on the ground of them, had not the churches and church teachers had good evidence that an Apostle wrote it. But we discover that the fourth Gospel was received in the second century without question or contradiction. The only exception is the opposition to it of a handful of so-called "Alogi," at Thyatira, about A.D. 170, who disliked it primarily on doctrinal grounds. But even this handful of sec-

The Alogi.

---

[1] For example, in Matt. xxiii. 37.
[2] For example, Matt. xi. 27 (Luke x. 22).

taries, by ascribing it to Cerinthus, a contemporary of John, the Apostle, at Ephesus, and an opponent, refuted themselves, since their assertion implied its early date, and since the acceptance by the church of Ephesus, and by the other churches in Asia Minor and elsewhere, of a Gospel which was the work of a notorious heretic, is incredible. To the testimony of Irenæus, and to the decisive character of it, in view of his relations to Polycarp and to others in that very region, we have already adverted.[1]

The fourth Gospel was written by a Palestinian Jew. This is shown, among other proofs, by peculiarities of language. Moreover, the Gospel is strewn with references to local peculiarities which prove the author to have been well acquainted with the scenes of the narrative. This characteristic has been admitted by prominent critics of the skeptical schools. Rénan says of the account of the healing of the nobleman's son in the fifth chapter, that it was written by one who had himself made the journey from Cana to Capernaum. Irenæus could not have been deceived in his recollections of what he had heard from Polycarp, a disciple of John, nor could he have been mistaken as to the person to whom Polycarp referred, and reminiscences of whom he was fond of relating. In the circle in the midst of which Polycarp was held in honor, and of which Irenæus, in

Local references.

[1] Page 48, seq.

his youth, was a member, there was no doubt or dispute respecting the authorship and date of the fourth Gospel.

The manner in which the authorship of the fourth Gospel is disclosed in the work itself contains a strong proof of its genuineness.

The author of the fourth Gospel—his disclosure of himself.

This disclosure of himself by the author stands in connection with an attestation appended to the book at the close. In the course of the narrative, a disciple is referred to repeatedly, but with an avoidance of the mention of his name. There leaned on the bosom of Jesus at the Last Supper "one of his disciples whom Jesus loved."[1] There went with Peter to the tomb of Jesus " the other disciple, whom Jesus loved."[2] He is spoken of as "another disciple," and "that other disciple." It will not be doubted that he was the "one of the two" who with Andrew followed Jesus to his abode.[3] It is said that on the second day after a certain occurrence he and Andrew were standing with John the Baptist, whose disciples they were. They heard what John said of Jesus as he walked by, and followed him. Jesus turned, and asked them what they were seeking. They inquired where his abode was. He invited them to come and see. It was four o'clock, we are told, when they joined him, and they spent with him the remainder of the afternoon. That this anony-

[1] xiii. 23. [2] xx. 2. [3] i. 39.

mous disciple was John, or that he is the person designated in these expressions, is not questioned. The "other disciple" was not Peter, for Peter is mentioned as an associate. No one has imagined it to be James, the brother of John, who died early in the Apostolic age.[1] Of the three who are known to have been most intimate with Jesus, only John is left. Now this covert method of revealing the author could only spring from a certain delicacy of feeling on his part, which prevented him from giving his own name, especially since he was led to speak of himself as standing in so tender a relation to Jesus. A forger, a writer pretending to be John, would never have resorted to this peculiar mode of indicating who he was, or professed to be. It is utterly contrary to the style characteristic of spurious writings.

At the end of the Gospel there is an attestation which has been connected with it, in all probability, since its first publication. It reads as follows: "This is the disciple which beareth witness of these things, and wrote these things; and we know that his witness is true."[2] According to the ancient tradition, the Gospel was published by the disciples of John at Ephesus, after his death. This, then, is the indorsement which comes from those into whose custody it was given.

Testimony of John's disciples.

If any should imagine that the Gospel was com-

[1] Acts xii. 2.   [2] John xxi. 24 (Revised Version).

posed by these pupils of John, on the basis of what they had learned from him, the objections to this hypothesis are conclusive. First, it is contrary to the certification just quoted. Secondly, it is conflated by the manner in which the author modestly veils his own personality, instead of directly declaring himself.

The style of the first of the Epistles ascribed to John makes it evident that it was written by the same author as the fourth Gospel. In this Epistle we have an unequivocal declaration that the author of it was with Jesus and an eye-witness of what he did.[1]

That the author was personally conversant with Jesus is distinctly implied in his use of the first person plural of the pronoun:[2] "We beheld his glory," etc. He plainly asserts that he saw water and blood flowing from the side of Jesus as he hung on the cross.[3] If it was not so, we are obliged to impute to the author, whoever he was, wilful deception.

The fourth Gospel is a sort of autobiography, or personal confession of the faith of the writer in Jesus, and of how it grew up in his soul. It is steeped in personal affection, and pervaded by the atmosphere of personal loyalty and devotion. All this involves the fact of personal intimacy and discipleship.

Personal intimacy implied.

It has been shown that the four Gospels were

[1] 1 John i. 1.   [2] John i. 14.   [3] xix. 34.

written by Apostles and well-informed contemporaries. Even if their authorship and date could not be definitely ascertained, there is good reason to believe that in their contents the story which the Apostles told of Jesus, his teaching and works, is fairly embodied. From Justin Martyr and other writers of the second century it is made plain that this and no other tradition existed on the subject. The opponents of Christianity knew of no other. One of the most acute of these was Celsus, who is supposed to have composed his attack about A.D. 180. From Origen's reply we can gather up a great portion of what Celsus wrote. Thus it is ascertained that the history of Jesus, which is the object of his adverse criticism, corresponds with what is narrated in the Gospels. Celsus knew of no other conception of Christ, and of his words and deeds.

Only one tradition.

Celsus.

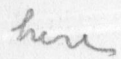

CHAPTER IX.

TRUSTWORTHINESS OF THE TESTIMONY OF THE APOSTLES.

We have before us in the Gospels the testimony of the Apostles. We have the substance of what they declared to be the truth respecting the career of Jesus. The question now to be considered is whether the Apostles are entitled to credit. They are worthy of belief unless it can be shown either that they intended to deceive, or were themselves mistaken. Were they impostors? Or, if not impostors, were they enthusiasts, incapable of discriminating between actual occurrences and their own imaginings? Were they knaves, or were they simpletons?

The alternative.

The Apostles understood that their office was that of witnesses. They were selected by Jesus to be with him, to hear what he said and to see what he did. In a passage, the authenticity of which is not open to question,[1] Peter requires that one should be chosen to take the place of Judas, who had been with them and with Christ.

Conscious of being witnesses.

---

[1] Acts i. 21-25. The prominence here given to Peter by the author, a Pauline Christian, prevents even skeptical critics from calling in question the truth of the historical statement.

He must be qualified to bear witness to the resurrection of Jesus—a fact singled out as the most important in the Apostles' testimony.

The Apostles never ceased to feel that they were disciples. They stood in the position, not of originators, but of learners. Something unspeakably precious had been communicated to them to be delivered to others. All their own hopes rested on the facts which they had nothing to do in originating.

<small>Always disciples.</small>

They tell their tale in the dispassionate tone that belongs to truthful witnesses. They are content to let the simple facts speak for themselves. For example, there are no invectives against Judas. They go no further than just to relate what he did.

<small>Their tone.</small>

The candor of the Apostles, and of the Evangelists who were not of their number, is evident. A single instance will suffice as an example. Luke relates how Paul was set upon by a furious mob of Jews.[1] They shouted that he had brought Greeks into the temple, and had defiled that "holy place." The historian takes pains to state immediately a fact—one that he might have suppressed—which was of the nature of an excuse for their violence. They had seen, he tells us, one Trophimus, an Ephesian, with Paul, and had heard that he had taken him into the temple.

<small>Their candor.</small>

[1] Acts xxi. 27 seq.

CREDIBILITY OF THE APOSTLES.

They show their honesty in relating things discreditable to themselves. Peter told the story of his denials of the Master, for it is related by Mark as well as by the other Evangelists. The reproofs of Jesus are faithfully set down. The Apostles speak of their ambition and contentious rivalry, and of the way in which they were rebuked by Christ.[1] They relate how they failed to understand Jesus in cases where it seemed obtuse in them not to take in his meaning.[2] What better proof can there be of candor? They even tell how they all forsook him.[3] It is evident that the Apostles had no thought of themselves, so absorbing was the interest which they felt in the scenes which they had beheld, and in which they had taken part, and in him to whom they looked up as to their lord and master. All personal considerations were lost in the magnitude of the events which had passed before their eyes.

Relate things to their own discredit.

The sincerity of the Apostles is proved by what they were willing to endure in consequence of the testimony which they gave. The Apostle Paul speaks of the Apostles collectively as "the off-scouring of all things."[4] They had no selfish advantage to gain. On the contrary, the hatred of their friends, exile, personal indignities hard to bear, even torture and death, were the

Their sincerity proved by their sufferings.

---

[1] Mark ix. 34; Luke ix. 46
[2] Matt. xv. 16, xvi. 6, 7, etc.
[3] Matt. xxvi. 56; Mark xiv. 50.
[4] 1 Cor. iv. 13.

reward which they had to expect for testifying to what they professed to have seen and heard.

The truth of the Gospel narratives is shown by a thousand incidental (and, therefore, undesigned) allusions to the topography, customs, and manners of the country—to peculiarities of time and place. These things, which prove their early date, confirm, also, their credibility.

<small>Allusions to local customs.</small>

That the Gospel narratives spring out of intentional deceit will not be seriously alleged. To account for them as far as they relate miracles, the "mythical theory" was proposed by Strauss. This theory was that groups of early believers in Jesus, brooding over Old Testament predictions of the Messiah and accounts of miracles wrought by the prophets, *imagined* that Jesus healed the sick, raised the dead, etc. These stories were an unconscious growth of fancy in secluded communities of Galilean followers of Jesus.

<small>The mythical theory.</small>

This theory is untenable. Where were the communities of Christians who were so far removed from the oversight of the Apostles? How could that childlike, unreflecting mood of feeling, required for the unconscious action of mythopœic fancy, arise or abide when the faith of Christian disciples was challenged at every turn, and when they were called upon to defend it against hostile criticism? How could those who thought that the Messiah *must* work miracles

<small>Objections to it.</small>

have been moved to believe in Jesus unless he actually met this indispensable condition? They felt that miracles there must be, we are told, and hence invented or dreamed out fictitious tales to fill the gap; and yet the lack of them had not stood in the way of their faith in the messianic claim of Jesus! The time between the death of Jesus and the composition of the Gospels was too short to admit of the rise of a body of myths, a spontaneous growth in the circles of believers. Moreover, the Gospels came not from secluded disciples, such as are imagined to have given birth to mythical tales. They came from the Apostles and those under their instruction and care. These considerations are conclusive; but, apart from them, the miracles, as we have seen, are so inseparably connected with the teaching of Jesus that neither ingredient of the Gospel narratives can be discarded while the other is saved. We cannot reject the accounts of miracles without, also, disbelieving the record of sayings of Christ, which are obviously and undeniably authentic.

An objection is made to the credibility of the Gospels on the ground of alleged discrepancies. Alleged discrepancies. The first thing to be said in answer to this objection is that whether these be real or only apparent, they prove that there was no collusion, no conspiracy, between the Evangelists or the informants from whom they, or any of them, derived their matter. The second remark is that

discrepancies and inaccuracies belong to human testimony generally. On the principle that a witness or an author is to be discredited if he fails of accuracy in all particulars, it would be impossible to believe anybody. Courts of law would have to be shut up, for the most veracious witnesses seldom agree in all the minutiæ which enter into their testimony. All books of history would have to be cast aside, including narratives written from personal observation. Paley says justly: "I know not a more rash or unphilosophical conduct of the understanding than to reject the substance of a story by reason of some diversity in the circumstances with which it is related. The usual character of human testimony is substantial truth under circumstantial variety. This is what the daily experience of courts of justice teaches. When accounts of a transaction come from the mouths of different witnesses, it is seldom that it is not possible to pick out apparent or real inconsistencies between them. These inconsistencies are studiously displayed by an adverse pleader, but often with little impression upon the minds of the judges." Where variations occur in testimony, or inaccuracies in any single witness or reporter, the only question is whether they are of such a number and character as to destroy the general trustworthiness of the narrators, and to cast doubts on the substantial contents of their tale. In the third place, whatever may be thought of minor points of variation from one another, the Gospels can be proved to contain no such instances of diversity in the narration as suffice to weaken their general credibility. It must be remembered that these books are not formal histories. They are memoirs. There is no aim at completeness. They are not put together by expert writers. Circumstances, even very important facts, may be left out of one and recorded by another. In narratives of this character there is often an appearance of contradiction where some additional circumstance, not introduced, would at once dispel this appearance.

It is sometimes made an objection to believing in the New Testament miracles that a great number of miraculous stories have been set afloat which are generally admitted to be fabulous. This objection overlooks the fact that the same thing is true of numberless narratives in which nothing miraculous is involved. Because there are so many instances of mistake or imposition, in what we read or hear, we do not disbelieve in everything that is related.

<small>Heathen and ecclesiastical miracles.</small>

The objection has no force unless it can be shown that the accounts of miracles which we feel justified in at once rejecting, are as well attested as are the miracles recorded in the Gospels. But this cannot be shown. It must be remembered that the circumstances under which testimony is given, as well as the temper and character of the witness, must be taken into view. The weight of proof is measured by the strength of both of these factors combined.

1. The Gospel miracles are expressly to verify revelation. It was, for the most part, only at marked epochs in the progress of divine revelation that, according to the Scriptures, miracles were wrought. On the contrary, alleged miracles outside of the Scriptures are frequently naked marvels, deriving no support from any high, distinctive purpose which they are to subserve.

2. The Gospel miracles were not wrought in coincidence with a prevailing system of belief, and for the furtherance of it. On the other hand, they were performed in behalf of teaching and of claims which were hostile to established prepossessions. The miracles of Jesus were a part of the means by which faith in him was created and built up. Miracles related by the ancient fathers, or in the mediæval legends, were in harmony with religious beliefs already deeply rooted. They were directly in the line of popular expectations. This is a difference of very great importance.

3. The disposition to deny the reality of the miracles wrought by Christ, or to explain them away, had to be confronted by the Apostolic witnesses. It has been said truly that "exorcism, which is the contemporary Jewish miracle referred to in the Gospels, is evidently, if it stands by itself, and is

not confirmed by other and more decided marks of divine power, a miracle of a most doubtful and ambiguous character." To whatever cause the disorder is referred, "a sudden, strong impression," rousing the energy of the patient, might, in less aggravated cases, effect a cure. But, even as to exorcism, the Jews recognized the difference in the cures effected by Jesus from anything familiar in their experience, and were driven to ascribe them to aid afforded by Beelzebub. In general, the miracles of Jesus were such as the people considered in the highest degree unlikely to occur. The statement, which is often made, that there was no idea of natural law, and, therefore, that there was an uninquiring credulity, is contrary to the truth. The idea of the stability of nature is constantly implied in the Gospel narratives. Galilee was a populous district, studded with cities and villages. The minds of the people were sharpened by trade and commerce. They were not illiterate barbarians. They were the countrymen of Josephus. There were superstitions then, as in every age since. But the difference between a natural event and a miracle was understood and felt. The common feeling is expressed in the words, "Since the world began was it not heard that any man opened the eyes of one that was born blind."[1] Nicodemus said: "No man can do these miracles that thou doest, except God be with him."[2] The

[1] John ix. 32.   [2] John iii. 2.

Pharisees and priests said: "Remember that that deceiver said, while he was yet alive, 'After three days, I will rise again.'"[1] Such a claim, they assumed, was characteristic of a *deceiver*. It was in the midst of such a community, in the face of all this disbelief, that the Apostles told their story.

4. They were subjected to the severe test of persecution and suffering. Was it facts that they affirmed? This was the question. Had there been a doubt in their minds, they must have given way under the pressure, not only of authority—the authority of the religious rulers and guides of the people—but, also, of the perils and sufferings which their testimony brought upon them.

5. The habit of mind of the Apostolic witnesses is essentially different from that of the narratives of heathen and ecclesiastical miracles, and of wonders elsewhere reported. Two things vitiate most of the testimony to events of this sort. The first is the lack of a clear perception of facts as they actually occur. The second is an appetite for the marvellous. This last feeling not only obscures the mental vision and is one cause of the fault just mentioned; it also begets a credulity which is fatal to the exercise of judgment respecting the statements of others. Both these defects, which are closely connected together, may coexist with many good traits, including piety. Now, in the

[1] Matt. xxvii. 63.

case of the Apostolic witnesses, what is remarkable is the sobriety of mind, which leaves the perceptions clear, and with it that conscientious regard for truth which insures strictly veracious testimony.

The dignity and simplicity of the miracles recorded in the New Testament are, as a rule, in strong contrast with those found in legendary tales. The miracles in the apocryphal Gospels are, as a class, grotesque, fantastic, or otherwise offensive. This is the prevailing character, for example, of the miracles described in the Gospel of the Infancy. The same character, although not always in so excessive a degree, belongs to heathen and mediæval legends. Exceptions occur, but they are exceptions—not numerous enough to efface the contrast between pagan and ecclesiastical miracles in general, and the miracles ascribed to Jesus in the Evangelists.

Finally, we revert to the character of Christ, which is too unique to be the product either of imagination or of conscious invention. When that character, in its immaculate purity, is contemplated, in connection with the declared purpose of his life and mission, "to bear witness to the truth," and "to seek and to save" the lost, supernatural manifestations of power appear to be a suitable accompaniment of his work in the world. Why not the power, as well as the holiness and love of God? The antecedent improbability of miracle vanishes.

CHAPTER X.

THE PROOF OF THE RESURRECTION OF JESUS FROM THE EVANGELISTS.

Now that the trustworthiness of the Gospel narratives has been established, we can appeal to the testimony to the resurrection of Jesus, which they present. We can reinforce the argument founded on the affirmations of the Apostle Paul, which was presented in a former chapter;[1] although Paul's testimony, even when considered by itself, warrants the conclusion that was drawn from it.

To the transcendent importance of this fact of the resurrection of Jesus, the Apostles were fully alive. They staked upon it their veracity. If he had not risen, they were willing to be considered false witnesses.[2] The Lord's resurrection was inseparably connected with the whole doctrine of redemption. It was involved in all their hopes of salvation from sin, and of future blessedness.[3] They went out to proclaim "Jesus and the resurrection."[4] The estimate which they put upon this central fact is adapted to inspire con-

Importance of the fact.

---

[1] Ch. VII.   [2] 1 Cor. xv. 15.   [3] 1 Cor. xv. 14.   [4] Acts xvii. 18.

fidence in the witness which they gave concerning it. They would take every precaution against mistake respecting a truth on which they were conscious that everything depended.

That Jesus really died is a proposition which it is no longer requisite to defend. If it were possible for him to survive the crucifixion, its prolonged torture, and the wound in the side, and if what appeared to be death could be supposed to have been only a swoon from which he awoke, how could his life in a mortal body have been continued? Where did he go? When did he really die? Such a continuation of his earthly life, if all other difficulties in the supposition were removed, could only have taken place through a consummate effort of deceit at which he himself connived.

<small>A real death.</small>

It is impossible to account for the alleged interviews of the Apostles with the risen Jesus, by the supposition that they were imaginary and grew out of an idea that, being the Messiah, he *must* rise from the tomb and appear in bodily form. There was not time for such a process of reasoning to take place in the minds of the Disciples, and for a series of visions, having no basis in reality, to spring out of it. It was on the morning of the third day that, as they affirmed, he appeared to them.¹ Nor can it be reasonably thought that real, miraculous visions of Jesus, parted from

<small>No hallucination.</small>

---

¹ 1 Cor. xv. 4; Mark xvi. 2, etc.

the body and entered on the heavenly life, were granted to them. This explanation is precluded by the fact that it was in his bodily form that they beheld him. It is absolutely excluded by the circumstances that attended his manifestations to them.

The empty tomb. The tomb, it must be remembered, was found empty, with the linen clothes left there, and the napkin folded and lying by itself.[1] The body could not have been carried off by the enemies of Christ. They would have produced it to confute the assertion that he had risen. It could not have been carried away and hidden by his friends, without a fraudulent intent on their part, which none at the present day would impute to them. But the final, unanswerable proof of the *The interviews.* resurrection is in the character of the interviews of Jesus with his followers. On the first Sunday there were five of these meetings with him. They were incredulous, but he overcame their incredulity. He spoke to them and they with him. He walked with them. He partook of food with them. They touched him. One of them put his finger upon the print of the nails.[2] The reality of his bodily presence was attested by what Luke justly calls "infallible proofs,"[3] appeals to the senses—appeals of such number and variety as rendered the idea of an illusion absurd.

[1] John xx. 2 seq.; Luke xxvi. 3, etc.   [2] John xx. 25 seq.
[3] Acts i. 3.

Add to these considerations a fact before adverted to. The manifestations of Jesus to the disciples were limited to a certain number of instances. The principal of these Paul refers to. A few others are related in the Gospels. All these interviews ceased after a limited, not very long time. Had they been the product of imagination and enthusiasm, they would have continued, increasing constantly the emotional excitement out of which they sprung. The ablest representative of the skeptical schools of criticism confesses that no explanation can be given of the undoubting and immovable faith of the Apostles in the resurrection of Jesus.[1] There is only one reasonable explanation—namely, that the fact occurred.

[1] F. C. Baur: History of the First Three Centuries, p. 39. He even calls the resurrection a "wunder" (miracle).

CHAPTER XI.

ALLEGED ERRORS OF THE APOSTLES IN MATTERS OF OPINION.

In answer to the objection that the Apostles held to erroneous opinions on certain subjects, it is to be said, in the first place, that no authority is claimed for the Apostles, and no superiority of knowledge, except on matters involved in their mission, or in the work specially assigned to them by Jesus. They did not themselves pretend that their knowledge of astronomy, or of other sciences, was beyond that of their Jewish contemporaries. In these particulars they may have been greatly excelled by many at that day.

Limits of their knowledge.

The objection has no force unless it refers to alleged errors in religious opinion. But even on this subject the objection is irrelevant unless it can be shown that the errors in question would invalidate their testimony to the facts which the Gospels record. If the question before us concerned the nature and limits of the *inspiration* of the Apostles, it would be necessary to consider it, but not where the inquiry is respecting the credibility of their testimony.

It may be well, however, to refer to some points

having a close relation to religion, and in regard to which it is said that the Apostles were in error.

Expectation of the second advent. One of these is the expectation of the speedy second coming of Christ. Let it be observed that they expressly affirm that the time of his second coming is not revealed. "Of that day and hour knoweth no man, not even the angels of heaven, neither the Son, but the Father only."[1] After the resurrection of Christ, when they asked him if he would then "restore the kingdom to Israel," he gave this comprehensive answer: "It is not for you to know times or seasons which the Father hath set within his own authority."[2] The decision of all these questions was reserved by the Father, and was not disclosed to man. We read in John's Gospel that Jesus, speaking of John, said to Peter: "If I will that he tarry till I come, what is that to thee?"[3] This occasioned a report "among the brethren" that John "should not die." But this misconstruction of what Jesus had said is corrected.[4] "Suppose," says Paley, "that this report had come down to us among the prevailing opinions of the early Christians, and that the particular circumstance from which the mistake sprang had been lost (which, humanly speaking, was most likely to have been the case), some at this day would have been ready to regard and quote the error as an

[1] Matt. xxiv. 36.
[2] Acts i. 7 (Revised Version).
[3] John xxi. 22.
[4] Verse 23.

impeachment of the whole Christian system." "To those who think that the Scriptures lead us to believe that the early Christians, and even the Apostles, expected the approach of the day of judgment in their own times, the same reflection will occur as that which we have made with respect to the more partial, perhaps, and temporary, but still no less ancient error, concerning the duration of St. John's life. It was an error, it may be likewise said, which would effectually hinder those who entertained it from acting the part of impostors." Those who think that the Apostles expected that Christ was to come soon, should not be surprised to find traces of this personal expectation in their writings. Nor ought they to be surprised if the influence of this idea is found to tinge the abbreviated reports of the predictive utterances of Christ which are presented in the Gospels.

Another difficulty in the New Testament narratives relates to what is said of demoniacs. It is represented that the souls of men were possessed by evil spirits, who inflicted on them physical distempers—epilepsy, lunacy, etc. The opinion has been adopted by not a few Christian scholars that the language of Christ on this subject was uttered simply by way of accommodation to a prevalent belief, and in order to effect the cure of those who were under the influence of it. In other words, he entered into the idea of the

Demoniacs.

persons thus afflicted with disease—humored the delusion, as it were—as a means of causing their recovery, and of assuring them of it. Their mistaken belief was harmless, from a religious point of view, and Christ was under no obligation to disabuse them of it, any more than to instruct them on the causes of disease in general, and to clear their minds of other medical delusions.

Christian scholars, to whom this solution is not satisfactory, are content to accept as real the fact of demoniacal possession at that epoch when the minds of men were oppressed and distracted by the inward conflict with evil. It was an extraordinary crisis in the spiritual life of individuals and of society. Too little is known of the supernatural world to warrant a dogmatic denial of the possibility of such an influence exercised by evil spirits.

On either of the views just stated, it remains true that the facts concerning the cure of the so-called demoniacs, of their actual deliverance from aggravated disorders, are authenticated by the testimony. The accounts in the Gospels of the healing of persons of this class are among the most graphic passages in these writings. They contain internal evidence of their verity. Of such a character is the narrative of the madman of Gadara, who cut himself with stones, and made his abode among the tombs. Conversations of Jesus, in connection with miracles of this

Testimony to the facts not weakened.

kind, conversations of unquestionable authenticity, prove the reality of the principal facts with which they are associated.

Difficulties are sometimes raised in reference to occasional interpretations of Old Testament pas-
Interpretation and reasoning. sages, which the Apostles introduce, or to certain arguments which they employ. Such difficulties, supposing them to be well-founded, do not affect the value of their testimony to facts. Some would contend that these difficulties have no ground to rest upon. Others would allow with Paley that we must "distinguish between their [the Apostles'] doctrines and their arguments. Their doctrines came to them by revelation, properly so called; yet in propounding these doctrines in their writings or discourses, they were wont to illustrate, support, and enforce them by such analogies, arguments, and considerations, as their own thoughts suggested." Paley quotes from Bishop Burnet this remark: "When divine writers argue upon any point, we are always bound to believe the conclusions their reasonings end in; but we are not bound to be able to make out, or even to assent to, all the premises made use of by them, in their whole extent, unless it appears plainly that they affirm the premises as expressly as they do the conclusions proved by them.[1]"

---

[1] Paley's Evidences, P. III. ch. II. Burnet's Exposition of the Articles, Art. 6.

CHAPTER XII.

ALLEGED DIFFICULTIES IN THE CONNECTION OF CHRISTIANITY WITH THE OLD TESTAMENT RELIGIOUS SYSTEM.

Objections are frequently made to Christianity on the ground of difficulties connected with the Old Testament, and with references to the Old Testament books in the New Testament.

That the religion of the Old Testament is recognized in the New as from God, and as having a divine sanction, distinguishing it from the religions of the Gentiles, is obvious. That Chris-

Genetic relation of Christianity to Judaism.

tianity has a genetic connection with the religion of the Jews, is a plain matter of history. And the contrast between the religion of the Jews and the religious systems of other nations, including those of the same stock—as the Babylonians—is an impressive proof that the sanction given to it by Jesus is well founded. The pure monotheism, the character ascribed to God, the teaching as to his moral and providential government, the spirit of devotion and of worship inspired by this system of faith, bear witness to its unique, supernatural source.

Jesus appealed to prophetical passages in the Old Testament, as pointing to the kingdom which he was to establish, and to the Messiah, its head. He disavowed, moreover, the intention to cast discredit on the prior revelations of law and duty, made in times of old, to Moses and the prophets. All this a Christian accepts both on the authority of Jesus as a teacher, and on account of its inherent reasonableness.

<small>Recognition of the Old Testament.</small>

But neither Christ nor the Apostles took up questions respecting the authorship and date of Old Testament writings—such questions as belong to historical and scholarly inquiry. Christ refused to act as an umpire in a dispute about an inheritance, saying: "Who made me a judge or divider over you?"[1] This shows how resolved he was to keep within the limits of his own distinctive calling, and not to step aside to perform offices, which, even if they were not unimportant, did not pertain to it. We have a right as Christians to rest on the declarations of Christ on questions respecting which he has pronounced judgment—questions on which he professed to speak "as one having authority." But we go too far when we stake the truth of Christianity on the correctness of opinions concerning which no verdict was intended to be pronounced by Christ or his Apostles.

<small>Limits of the teaching of Jesus.</small>

[1] Luke xii. 14.

But Christ did teach emphatically the gradualness of divine revelation, and the consequent imperfection of religious knowledge, and of the knowledge of duty under the old dispensation. There was a Mosaic law respecting divorce, which fell short of the Christian ideal. It was given, Christ taught, on account of the hardness of heart of the people, who were prepared for nothing better.[1] He substituted for it another, more stringent enactment. John the Baptist, he said, was inferior to no prophet; yet the least Christian disciple was greater than he—was possessed of more light, and stood on a higher plane as regards the perception of God's plans and ways.[2] The recollection of the *gradualness* of the revelation of God and of religious truth sets aside at once numerous difficulties which have been alleged respecting the teaching of the Old Testament Scriptures, as well as concerning the lives and the character of persons described and commended in them.

The gradualness of divine revelation.

In truth, the connection of the faith of Israel with Christianity most impressively indicates the divine origin of the religion of Jesus. We behold the long course of this historical movement—starting in the remote past, flowing onward, like a river, through all the centuries before Christ, until there it widens into a sea that spreads more and more, as the ages succeed

The plan of history.

[1] Matt. xix. 8; Mark x. 5.   [2] Matt. xi. 11; Luke vii. 28.

one another, over the surface of the globe. As the birth of Christ divides history into two parts, so his coming furnishes the clue to the understanding of it. His offices of love and mercy to the race unveil the purpose of God, the interpretation of his plan, as regards mankind, including Jew and Gentile, both before and since the SAVIOUR OF THE WORLD appeared. To each branch of the human race, to each of the nations of the earth, Providence assigned the place and the period of its existence, guiding and training all, to the end that they might seek after God, and fulfil, each its allotted part, in the world-wide kingdom which Christ was sent to establish.

CHAPTER XIII.

PROOF OF CHRISTIANITY FROM PROPHECY.

Prophecy is a species of miracle. There are limits to the power of human foresight. The field beyond is open to conjecture, but is excluded from trustworthy prediction. Prophecy which is fulfilled under circumstances that forbid the supposition of mere coincidence or accident, and the supposition that it causes its own fulfilment through some influence exerted by it, necessarily involves supernatural agency. Nothing else can account for the conformity of the event with the prediction. If it could be shown respecting one who utters predictions that in some instances they fail of accomplishment, even then the cases in which they are verified, provided they cannot be resolved into fortunate guesses, prove that at certain times, or to a certain degree, he is gifted with superhuman foresight.

Nature of the argument.

The Old Testament contains a large predictive element. It might be said with truth that a stream of prophecy runs through the Old Testament Scriptures. The religious guides of the Hebrew people ever looked forward to a grand future for which the present was only a prepa-

Prophecy pervasive in the Old Testament.

ration. There are three striking particulars in which this prophetic character of Old Testament teaching, and of the devotional utterances connected with it, appears. First, there is to be a great improvement in the religion itself. It is to take on a purer, more spiritual form.[1] Secondly, it is to have a world-wide predominance.[2] The heathen nations are to embrace it, or to be brought under its sway. The whole earth is to acknowledge Jehovah. Thirdly, this spread and domination of the Old Testament religion is to be secured by the Messiah. A great leader, guide, prince is to appear, under whom the kingdom of God is to become universal. Righteousness and blessing are to attend its progress. The prophetic pictures vary in form. Elements derived from the kingdom of the Jews and from their religion in its then existing form naturally colored the anticipations and mingled in the visions of the seer and the saint. But these subordinate features, in which prophecy varies from actual experience or accurately written history, do not lessen the profound impression which these predictive declarations of the Old Testament, viewed in connection with what we know of Christ and of Christianity, are adapted to make. The insight of the prophets into the plan of God has been verified in the events of subsequent ages, down to the present time.

[1] Jeremiah xxxi. 31-35.   [2] Is. ii. 2, etc.

There was a class of prophets among the Hebrews. To foretell future events was only an incidental, it was not the principal, function of their office. They professed to be called of God to instruct, to encourage, and to warn the people. They spoke with an eloquence which made men feel that they were animated by an influence from above, and that God spoke through them. This was true, for example, of the Prophet Isaiah. A part of their predictions cover the points referred to in the preceding remarks. The coming perfection and glory of the kingdom, and of the Messiah its head, was their theme. But, besides these prophecies of a more general nature, there were uttered, in special exigencies, predictions of particular events in the near or more distant future. They were prophecies which did not spring from any statesmanlike sagacity or power of forecast. The prophets might be called from humble vocations in life. Amos was a herdsman. The prophetic insight, or foresight, went beyond the possible reach of human calculation. An instance of prophecy of the kind here referred to is the predictions of Isaiah respecting the rapidly approaching downfall of the kingdoms of Israel and Syria, which had concluded an alliance with each other, and of the failure of their project against Judah.[1] Another instance is Isaiah's prophecy of the failure of the powerful

[1] Isaiah vii.

army of the Assyrian king, Sennacherib, in his siege of Jerusalem.[1] Among the prophecies respecting the Messiah and his work, the passage in Isaiah concerning the servant of God is remarkable.[2] It contains verses which cannot refer to the people as a body, or to the pious kernel of the nation. Of such a character is verse 6: "All we have gone astray; we have turned every one to his own way; and the Lord hath laid on him the iniquity of us all." The prophecy has reference to one individual, and its correspondence to the experience of Christ is close. That Jesus himself foretold the coming destruction of Jerusalem is proved by the testimony of the first three Evangelists. More impressive than the prediction of any single event is the foreknowledge he had of the spread of the Gospel and of the victory of his kingdom. It was to grow like the mustard-seed, and to spread its influence like the hidden leaven.

[1] Isaiah xxxvii. 21 seq.   [2] Isaiah lii. 13–liv.

CHAPTER XIV.

ARGUMENT FOR CHRISTIANITY FROM THE CONVERSION AND THE CAREER OF THE APOSTLE PAUL.

About four years after the crucifixion, Saul of Tarsus, a man of great ability and sincerity, who belonged to the sect of the Pharisees, was trained in a rabbinical school at Jerusalem, and was zealous in persecuting Christian disciples, was converted, and became the principal agent in planting the Gospel in the cities of the Roman Empire. His conversion was sudden. "It pleased God," he says, "to reveal his Son in me, that I might preach him among the heathen."[1] The particulars of his conversion, when he was on the road to Damascus, on an errand of persecution, are related by Luke in the Acts. Miraculous circumstances attended it.[2]

It is impossible to account for this event by merely natural causes. The only theory of this nature which has been advanced is the one to which we have adverted on a preceding page[3]—the theory of hallucination. But, as we have said, his was not the state of mind out of which an illusion of this sort could be engendered. He expressly states

His state of mind.

[1] Gal. i. 16. [2] Acts ix. 2 seq., xxii. 5 seq. [3] Page 83.

that he had no misgivings in regard to the rectitude of the course he was pursuing. "*I verily thought with myself* that I ought to do many things contrary to the name of Jesus of Nazareth."¹ He had been a persecutor, he tells us, but found mercy because he "did it ignorantly, in unbelief."² He was, to be sure, engaged in a hard, wearisome struggle to live up to his idea of legal righteousness. The yoke of the law pressed heavily upon him. This was a silent, unconscious preparation for the relief which the Gospel was to afford; but the immediate effect of this conscientious legalism was not to excite in him the least favor to the Christian cause, the least inclination to regard Jesus as the Messiah. The effect, on the contrary, was to increase his zeal in putting down what he considered a wicked and baneful heresy. As we have remarked, the expression, "It is hard for thee to kick against the pricks," does not imply, or remotely suggest, the presence in his mind of compunction or inward opposition to the work in which he was engaged. It was a proverbial expression, signifying that he was embarked in a futile enterprise—one that would not avail to crush the cause of Christ, but would, the longer he persevered in it, harm himself the more. The metaphor was taken from the conflict of oxen with the driver behind them, and their vain attempt to resist him by kicking against the goad.

[1] Acts xxvi. 9.   [2] 1 Tim. i. 13

PROOF FROM THE CONVERSION OF PAUL. 101

To say that the occurrence which turned Paul from an ardent enemy to a devoted friend of the cause of the Gospel was only "a vision" explains nothing. If it were only a vision it would be necessary to show how a vision of that character could take place, save by supernatural agency. But it has been explained how the Apostle distinctly implies that the perception which he had of Christ at his conversion was of an entirely different character from the disclosures which he subsequently had in apocalyptic visions.[1]

<small>Was it a "vision"?</small>

Besides the miracle involved, the conversion of Paul was a wonderful transformation of character. His whole aim in life was changed. Along with this revolution of purpose there arose within him new tempers of heart—the spirit of humility and love, of patience and forgiveness; in a word, the spirit of Christ.

<small>Change of character.</small>

The result of that incident on the road to Damascus was the marvellous career of Paul as a preacher of Christianity, and a most remarkable and successful propagator of the faith which he had been trampling under foot. How different would the history of Europe have been, how different the history of mankind, had the labors of Paul as an apostle of the Cross never been performed!

It is important to add that the Apostle Paul himself wrought miracles. We have his word for it,

[1] 1 Cor. xv. 8.

and no one doubts his truthfulness. In the Epistle to the Romans, he explicitly refers to "the mighty signs and wonders" which Christ had wrought by him.[1] So he reminds the Corinthians, in his Second Epistle to them, of "the signs and wonders and mighty deeds" which had been wrought by him before their eyes.[2] They were "signs" of "the Apostle;" that is, of the Apostolic office. Now we find that the direction to work miracles was in the commission given by Christ to the Apostles.[3] It cannot reasonably be doubted that the miracles of Paul and of the other Apostles were consciously done in pursuance of this commission. It is safe to conclude that Jesus himself professed to work miracles, and that the Apostles, in this particular, had not only his precept, but his example before them.

Miracles.

[1] Rom. xv. 19.   [2] 2 Cor. xii. 12.
[3] Matt. x. 1, 8; Mark iii. 15, etc.

CHAPTER XV.

PROOF OF THE DIVINE ORIGIN OF CHRISTIANITY FROM THE INTRINSIC EXCELLENCE OF THE CHRISTIAN SYSTEM.

In paving the way for the consideration of the evidence for miracles, prominent peculiarities of Christianity, including the character of Jesus, were touched upon. Brief additional observations will here be made on leading features of the Gospel.

The Christian conception of God represents him as a being who unites with infinite power and wisdom the moral attributes of holiness and love. He does not, as in the creed of Deism, stand apart from the world, nor is he, as in the creed of Pantheism, identified with it. He is immanent in the world, present with his all-pervading energy, "not far from any one of us," yet personal, acquainted with all our thoughts, and hearing prayer. Man is declared to be made in the image of God, and qualified, therefore, for conscious intercourse and fellowship with him. Moral evil is not confounded with physical evil, or made its product, but is traced back to the voluntary separation of mankind from God, and to the consequent rule in their

God.

Man.

Sin.

nature of propensities which ought to be kept subordinate. In the recovery of mankind, "the axe is laid at the root of the tree." In the Restorer, Jesus Christ, God is manifested, and, at the same time, the ideal of human perfection is realized. God is re-connected with mankind. Reconciliation is effected in a way that brings no cloud upon the holiness of the divine character and government. In Christ, the life of communion with the divine Father, and of peace in that relation, is maintained in the conflict with temptation, in the face of the world's hatred, and on the cross. That inward life is communicated to all who are attracted to him as disciples and followers. It is nourished within them by the invisible Spirit, replacing his visible presence. In the new relation to Christ, and through him to the Father, they detach themselves from every earthly object regarded as an idol, or an indispensable good, and thus gain strength to endure "the loss of all things." They form a community of the children of God, drawing within itself all who aspire after the life of sonship and of oneness with the Father. Life on the earth becomes a school for the training of the soul for a higher state of existence in the future. To them, all suffering is the chastisement of a Father, and death is a door of access to a heavenly abode. The entire course of events, including the most minute, is ordered of

God, so that all things work together for good to them that love him.

To use the world, and not abuse it, to enjoy the world without being a slave to it, is the Christian's privilege. An excessive value is to be attached to no form of earthly happiness; but, on the other hand, asceticism, together with a cynical contempt for human relations and pleasures, is equally precluded.

The Gospel not ascetic.

Christianity is a religion of principles, not of rules. In the room of specific and minute precepts, it sets forth the great ends with reference to which conduct is to be shaped. But within these bounds the individual is left, for the most part, to be guided by his own intelligence and moral sense. The aim is to mould aright the leading motives of action, so that a man shall be a law to himself, and spontaneity shall take the place of legal restraint. The supreme law is affirmed to be love, than which no higher or more comprehensive principle of action can be imagined. Discipleship is not a literal imitation of Christ, a copying of his particular actions, but rather the living appropriation of his spirit. No type of goodness more worthy can be conceived of than the one presented in the actual life of Jesus.

Christianity a religion of principles.

Christianity is adapted to be the religion of the world. It has all the requisites of a universal religion. It teaches the equality of the race before

God, the brotherhood of mankind, the common depravity of men, and the consequent common need of forgiveness and of deliverance from sin. The salvation provided in the Gospel is suited, not to any single nation or to any branch of the human family exclusively, but equally to every member of the race. In the community of Christ there is neither Greek nor Jew, bond nor free, male nor female.[1] The "good news" of the love of God to the ill-deserving is to be carried to "every creature." With the proclamation of human guilt and sin, there are carried the tidings of an atonement, of pardon, of the means of purification.

Christianity adapted to mankind.

Can a religion having this lofty character and this adaptation to the world be attributed to the Galilean laborers who were concerned in the first teaching of it? Can it be considered as the offspring of merely human purity and wisdom?

[1] Gal. iii. 28; Col. iii. 11.

CHAPTER XVI.

PROOF AFFORDED BY THE CONTRAST OF CHRISTIANITY WITH OTHER RELIGIONS AND WITH PHILOSOPHICAL SYSTEMS.

Christianity, when it is compared with the other religions of the world, is seen to be the one true, or absolute religion. It is free from the defects that belong to them. It supplies the elements which are missing in them. It fills out what is wanting in an inchoate system, true in its foundations, but incomplete, as was the religion of the Old Testament.

The religion of the ancient Persians, the worshippers of light, who professed to derive their faith *The Zoroastrian religion.* from Zoroaster, divided the empire of the world between two antagonistic deities. The creed was dualism, a theory that also mingles itself in the Pantheistic religions of India. Confucius, the sage of China, was a moral-*Confucius.* ist. He was the author of ethical and political precepts not without value, but he made no claim to reveal things invisible. It is often said that the golden rule is found in Confucius. But in *Originality of the Gospel.* him, and in every other ethnic writer to whom it is ascribed, it occurs either in a negative form, or merely in some particular relation—for example, as defining the duty of the parent to the child. The same thing is true of the golden rule as it is found in the Rabbis. Two or three sentences of the Lord's Prayer appear to have existed in earlier Jewish forms of devotion. The originality of Jesus is seen in the addition of these to the other petitions, and the union of all in a living whole; just as the golden rule acquires a deeper meaning when it is coupled with his teaching on what man ought to desire for himself and to count as the true good. But the originality of the Gospel lies especially in the relation of its moral precepts to religious doctrine, and to the new life which is implanted through the connection of the believer with Christ.

The only two religions, besides the religion of Christ, which can pretend to the character of univer-

Mohammedanism.

sality, are Mohammedanism and Buddhism. Mohammedanism derived its materials from Rabbinical sources, and thus, indirectly, from the Old Testament revelation. In its earnest faith in the unity of God, and in its protest against idolatry, it was in sympathy with the teaching of the Bible. In these doctrines, heartily embraced, lay the secret of the power of Islam, as far as that power was legitimate. But there were two grand defects in its theology. There was no such exaltation of the love of God, the highest attribute of his character, as the Bible contains; and there was no room for the unfolding of a grander future.

such as the Messianic hope of the Old Testament involved. The moral code of Islam includes a sanction of polygamy and slavery. The desire of sensual gratification enters into the hope of paradise, and this reward is held out as one motive to the believer. Under Mohammedanism, woman can never rise above a degraded condition, or approach that equality with man which Christianity has secured for her. Mohammedanism is a religion to be propagated by force, the employment of which for the overcoming of error Christianity forbids. It is, moreover, the religion of the letter. The disciple is forever bound to observe all the special precepts of the Koran. There is only a nominal and ignorant recognition of Christ. The elevating and consoling influences which, to the Christian mind, connect themselves with the name of Jesus, are wanting in the creed of the Mohammedan devotee.

Owing to these characteristics of Islam it is not capable of advancing the nations that embrace it beyond a certain stage of progress. There civilization, all that pertains to the higher life of man, is petrified in immovable forms, or gives way to decrepitude and decay.

Buddhism inculcated certain virtues. It enjoined self-conquest and universal kindness. It laid down a number of special precepts which resemble injunctions of the New Testament. But these moral rules are linked in Buddhism with

Buddhism.

a system of Pantheism and with the exhortation to renounce the desire of a future life. The doctrine of "Karma" involves no such thing as continued personal identity and immortality. Nirvana, the state of bliss, is tranquillity here, and extinction, as far as identity of consciousness is concerned, hereafter. Buddhism promised a release from the burdens of caste and the dread of transmigration. This negative good was the boon which it offered, and accounts for its progress in the land of its origin. But the Buddhistic religion brought in an ascetic, a monkish system hardly less fruitful of misery than the two-fold curse which it aimed to displace. "In it we have an ethical system but no lawgiver, a world without a creator, a salvation without eternal life, and a sense of evil but no conception of pardon, atonement, reconciliation, or redemption."[1]

In ancient times there were systems of philosophy which sought to afford light and solace to the minds of men. Socrates, the best of the heathen teachers, although he believed in a supreme Deity, still held also to "lords many and gods many," and mingled with the hope of another life an admixture of doubt. He felt the need of some sure "word of God" to guide us in the right way.[2] Plato taught that virtue is likeness to God according to the measure of human power; but his concep-

Philosophy.

Socrates.

Plato.

---
[1] T. W. Rhys Davids, in Non-Christian Religions, p. 131.　[2] Apol. 21.

CHRISTIANITY AND OTHER SYSTEMS. 111

tion of God, both as to his natural and moral attributes, fell decidedly below that of Christian theism. Moreover, to the question how to attain to such a resemblance to God, how to conquer the evil within us, he could give no satisfactory answer. He mistook the source of moral evil, which he made to be chiefly ignorance; and philosophy, which he conceived of as the proper remedy for such a malady, he held that only a few were competent to understand. The two systems most in vogue when the Gospel was first preached in the Roman Empire were Epicureanism and Stoicism. It was Epicureans and Stoics who encountered the Apostle Paul at Athens.[1] The Epicureans disconnected the gods from all concern with the affairs of men. They were practically atheists. They made the sum of human virtue to be a self-regarding prudence. Stoicism was a nobler system. It enjoined, as the source of peace, resignation to the divine will; but that divine will was indistinguishable from fate, and the repose of mind of the Stoic sage was gained at the cost of quelling and chilling the natural emotions. In the room of fellowship with Zeus, the Supreme One, the thing aimed at was an independence of Zeus, a proud self-reliance. Suicide was held to be lawful, and might be expedient; for notwithstanding all that was said of the wise order of the world, there

The Epicureans.

The Stoics.

[1] Acts xvii. 18.

were situations, it was thought, when a man was bound by self-respect to put an end to his own life. In the Stoic system, there was no rational motive for the existence of the world. There was no good to be attained by the divine Providence of which the Stoic spoke; for all things were to issue in a universal conflagration.

In contrast with all the ancient systems of philosophy, Christianity brought forward such a conception of God that the precept to be like him was intelligible and could be profitably obeyed. It brought forward the truth of a Providence of God, extending over all persons and events, a universal care comprehending the least of God's creatures, and causing all things to conspire to promote the well-being of his children. Natural sensibility is not petrified. Natural emotions and affections are left in healthy activity, but trust in the fatherly love and wisdom of God enables the afflicted to be at peace. Moreover, in distinction from all other religions and philosophies, Christianity provides redemption. That is to say, while it holds up the ideal of perfection, the law of righteousness, it provides, at the same time, effectual means of attaining, through Jesus Christ, to the partial, and ultimately to the complete, realization of it.

Christianity and philosophy.

When the incomparable superiority of the Christian system over the other religions of the world and over the highest achievements of philosophy is duly appreciated, it appears unreasonable to think that Christianity sprang from the unaided intelligence of the humble, unlettered Hebrews who were the instruments of publishing its truths to the world.

8

CHAPTER XVII.

CORROBORATIVE PROOF OF THE TRUTH OF CHRISTIANITY FROM ITS UTILITY.

As pernicious tendencies and consequences would prove that a religion is false, so a demonstrated beneficence is evidence, not without weight, that the system of religion having this tendency and effect is true. It is said of certain heathen religions and of Mohammedanism that they are productive of good. This is conceded up to a certain degree. This result may be attributed to elements of truth which they contain. But Christianity differs in being useful without any drawback, and to an extent wholly without parallel.

Christ styled his followers "the light of the world" and "the salt of the earth." This they
Light and Life. proved themselves to be. They failed then, as afterwards, to live up to the standard of Christian character and conduct. Nevertheless, Christianity illuminated the world, pouring a flood of light on man and his relations to God, on human duties, and the design and issues of our life on earth. And Christianity powerfully and effectu-

ally counteracted the tendencies to demoralization and ruin. It rescued society from the decay and moral putrefaction into which it was rapidly sinking. In the midst of a falling world, it planted the seeds of a better civilization.

Christianity asserted the incalculable worth of every human soul. It declared that no individual *Effects of Christianity.* is made to be the mere instrument of another's gratification. The welfare of every individual is an end in itself. Hence the Gospel insisted on the equality of all men before God. At the same time, self-sacrifice was made the supreme duty and was declared to be the source of the highest blessedness to him who practises it. These principles were the foundation of liberty and the fountain of beneficence. Not only was the ideal of virtue set forth; new, inspiring motives to the practice of it were presented in the mission and example of Jesus. The result of the influence of Christianity was the purification of domestic life. The rigor of paternal authority was softened. The wife and mother was elevated to her true place. Christianity has raised woman from degradation. It has improved, in a corresponding measure, the lot of children. It has immeasurably improved the condition of the laboring classes, by insisting that they shall have their just dues. The poor and unfortunate became objects of compassion and recipients of practical aid in multiform ways. Christianity promoted civil liberty. It inculcated loyalty, but put an end to the unqualified domination of the State. While the magistrate was to be obeyed as the minister of God, he was to be disobeyed if he enjoined anything against the divine law. The process began of conforming civil law to the requirements of justice. "Stranger" was no longer the synonym of "enemy." International law has taken on a new character under the influence of the Christian religion, in which are recognized the rights of nations, even the weakest. The spirit of charity, no longer confined by the bounds of nation and kindred, embraces all mankind. Such were the inherent tendencies, and such has been the actual power of Christianity, that its effect on the individual was properly styled "a new creation."[1] One looking at the influence of Christianity in the first centuries after it appeared, and in the ages following to the present time, sees the result of that revolution in personal character, of which the Apostle said: "The old things are passed away; behold, they are become new."

The transforming effect of Christianity is the miracle of history. A religion adequate to the production of such beneficent results must have God for its author.

[1] 2 Cor. v. 17 (Revised Version).

CHAPTER XVIII.

CORROBORATIVE PROOF OF CHRISTIANITY FROM ITS RAPID SPREAD IN THE FIRST CENTURIES.

The rapid progress of a religion may be owing to the indulgence granted by it to immoral practices, or to the use of force in the dissemination of it. In this way the victories of Islam are partly to be accounted for. Or the spread of a religion may be caused by the hope inspired of a deliverance from grievous burdens imposed by a religious system previously dominant, even although the new faith is not, on the whole, of an ennobling character. This explains the progress of Buddhism in India; while the ready junction or identification of Buddhism with the existing religions of China and Japan gave it a free course in those countries.

To neither of these causes was the surprising conquest of the Roman Empire by the Christian faith
Self-denial required.
due. It was at variance with the selfish, national ambition of the Jews, with their tenacious clinging to their ritual, and with their bigoted assumption of superiority over every other people. The Gospel demanded of the heathen the

renunciation of all their objects of worship, of all the employments and amusements that involved participation in the ancestral and legal forms of devotion. More than this, it required inexorably the forsaking of every species of immorality, and the subjugation of every desire for forbidden pleasures. It was supported by no influential class—not by the rich, or learned, or those holding high social or official stations. By these generally, it was regarded with disdain. Christians were objects of popular contempt. Soon severe laws were enforced against them, and they became victims both of legal and of mob violence. To become a Christian was to expose one's self to the "loss of all things." Yet notwithstanding all these requirements and all these exposures, Christianity continued to make converts rapidly, until it became clear that Roman imperial authority was not strong enough to extirpate the new faith or to stay its advance. At length, in the space of a few centuries, the altars of heathenism were deserted, and the last vestiges of heathen worship passed away.

The proximate causes of this rapid progress, Gibbon makes to be five: The zeal of the early Christians, which he represents to have been derived from the Jews, but to have been purged of Jewish narrowness; the doctrine of a future life of rewards and punishments; the power of working miracles, ascribed to the

<small>Gibbon on the progress of Christianity.</small>

primitive Church; the pure and austere morals of the Christians, and the union and discipline of the Christian republic—the ecclesiastical community. But these causes are distinct from one another. How, it has been pertinently asked, did they come to be combined in the same persons? How shall we account for this coincidence? How, for example, did zeal come to be cleared of narrowness? and how happened this ardor, mixed with liberality, to be associated with the Christian doctrine respecting the future life? Then it is obvious that these causes are, one and all, the effect of Christianity—ingredients of the Gospel or its natural consequences. The solution, therefore, amounts to this, that the cause of the rapid diffusion of Christianity was Christianity itself, or qualities inhering in it.

This is in effect the solution of a more recent writer who has undertaken to make clear the causes of the conversion of Rome.[1] It was not the alleged miracles; it was not, in any considerable degree, the reasoning from prophecy, which achieved the great conquest.[2] It was "the elements of power and attraction" which the new religion combined. These were its freedom from "local ties;" its strong appeal to the affections; its "pure and noble system of ethics;" its doctrine of the brotherhood of man, and of "the supreme sanctity of love." To the

---

[1] Lecky: History of European Morals from Augustus to Charlemagne, vol. i., p. 409 seq. [2] P. 409.

philosopher it was at once "the echo of the highest ethics of the later Stoics, and the expansion of the best teaching of the school of Plato." To a world weary of lower ideals, Christianity presented "an ideal of compassion and love—an ideal destined for centuries to draw around it all that was greatest, as well as all that was noblest upon earth—a Teacher who could weep by the sepulchre of his friend, who was touched with the feeling of our infirmities."[1] "The chief cause of its success was the congruity of its teaching with the spiritual nature of mankind." "It planted its roots so deeply in the hearts of men," "because it corresponded with their religious wants, aims, and emotions, because the whole spiritual being could then expand and expatiate under its influence." The author who has thus traced the early triumph of Christianity mainly to its own inherent, exalted characteristics, leaves unsolved the problem of the origin of a system whose power sprang from its transcendent worth. Those who believe, with a living faith, in a personal God will not find it unreasonable to accept the explanation which the New Testament presents, and refer this world-transforming Gospel to divine revelation.

[1] P. 412.

INDEX.

ACTS, genuineness of the, 62
Alogi, 64
Apostles, the, not victims of hallucination, 44; their trustworthiness, 70 seq.; their candor, 71 seq.; their sobriety, 79; tested by sufferings, 79; their alleged errors in doctrine, 86 seq.; their views on the Second Advent, 85; their interpretations and reasonings, 90

BARNABAS, the Epistle of, its quotations from Matthew, 55
Baur, F. C., 85
Buddhism, 109
Burnet, Bishop, 90
Byron, 24

CELSUS, 69
Christ, his character, 32, 81; his perfection, 35; not self-deceived, 36; his sanction of the Old Testament religion, 92; limits of his teaching, 92. See "Resurrection"
Christianity, the needs met by it, 25 seq.; admitted facts of, 28; its rapid spread, 29; its influence, 30; its divine origin shown by the character of Christ, 32; its leading features, 103 seq.; a religion of principles, 105; a religion for the world, 106; contrasted with other systems, 107 seq.; proof from its utility, 114 seq.; proof from its rapid spread, 117 seq.
Church, the Christian, its rise, 30

DEMONIACS, 86

EPICUREANISM, 111
Evidence, historical, its nature, 4; probable and demonstrative, 5; cumulative, 5; internal and external, 6; the affections, a source of, 7

GENUINENESS of a book, its meaning, 3
Gibbon, on the spread of Christianity, 118
God, his benevolence, 24
Gospels, their genuineness, 47 seq.; Irenæus respecting the,

48 seq.; Justin Martyr's use of them, 50 seq.; Tatian's use of them, 53; references to them in Polycarp, 54; in "The Teaching," etc., 55; the witness of the ancient versions to the, 56; internal evidence for the, 60 seq.; local references in the, 61; mystical theory respecting the, 73; alleged discrepancies in the, 74; their testimony to the resurrection of Christ, 82 seq. See the Gospels severally

HORACE, 24
Hume, his argument against miracles, 15 seq.
Huxley, on Hume's argument, 17

INSPIRATION, what is it? 2
Irenæus, his witness to the Gospels, 48 seq.; his relation to Polycarp, 49, 65

JEWS, their religion, 28
John the Baptist, 28; performed no miracles, 40
John, the Gospel of, used by Justin, 53; its relation to the first three Gospels, 63; local references in, 65; the author's way of disclosing himself, 66; attestation at the end of, 67; not written by disciples of John, 68; a kind of autobiography, 68. See "Gospels"
Josephus, 28
Justin Martyr, his witness to the Gospels, 50 seq.; to John's Gospel, 53

LECKY, on the early progress of Christianity, 119
Luke, an attendant of Paul, 61
Luke, the writings of, 61. See "Gospels" and "Acts"

MARK, the Gospel of, Papias on, 57. See "Gospels"
Matthew, the Gospel of, quoted in Barnabas, 55; Papias on 57. See "Gospels"
Mill, J. S., his comment on Hume's argument, 16
Miracles, definition of, 9; terms for, in the New Testament, 10; not without a cause, 11; Hume's argument against, 15; prove design, 18; can evil spirits perform them? 18; their relation, as proofs, to doctrine, 18; the sinlessness of Jesus, one of them, 35; presupposed in the teaching of Christ, 37 seq.; heathen and ecclesiastical, 76 seq.; wrought by Paul, 101
Mohammedanism, 108
Mythical theory, 73

OLD TESTAMENT system, its relation to Christianity, 91; its prophetic character, 95 seq.

PALEY, 75, 90; on the need of Revelation, 22
Papias, his account of Mark and Matthew, 57
Paul, his witness to the resurrection of Jesus, 41 seq.; his conversion, miraculous, 42 seq., 99 seq.; wrought miracles, 101
Plato, 110

INDEX.

Polycarp, his relation to Irenæus, 49, 65; quotes from Matthew and John, 54

Presumption, logical, its meaning, 21

Prophecy, proof from, 95 seq.

RÉNAN, 37, 65

Resurrection of Jesus, testimony of Paul respecting it, 41 seq.; proved from the Evangelists, 82 seq.

Revelation, antecedent probability of, 22; the need of, 23 seq.; the need of, met by Christianity, 25

SOCRATES, 110

Stoicism, 111

Strauss, D. F., 37, 73

TATIAN, his "Diatessaron," 53

"Teaching of the XII Apostles," as a witness to the Gospels, 55

UNIFORMITY of nature, 13

VERSIONS, the ancient, their witness to the Gospels, 56

ZOROASTER, 107

CHRISTIAN EVIDENCES AND HOMILETICS.

MANUAL OF CHRISTIAN EVIDENCES. By Prof. GEORGE PARK FISHER, D.D., LL.D., Professor of Ecclesiastical History in Yale College. 16mo, 75 cents.

The aim of the book is to present the Evidences of Christianity in a concise, lucid form, for the benefit of those who have not the leisure to study extended treatises on the subject. It is intended both for private reading and for the use of classes in public institutions. Although brief, it includes a distinct statement of both the internal and external proofs. The arguments are shaped to meet objections and difficulties which are felt at the present time, and the historic evidence is carefully confined to the present state of scholarship and learning.

THE EXAMINER.—"It is worth its weight in gold. It is by all odds the best treatise on the Evidences of Christianity for general use that we know. It is sound, judicious, clear, and scholarly."

THE N. Y. SUN.—"Compact, thorough, and learned, its simplicity of style and brevity ought to commend it to a wide circle of readers."

THE GROUNDS OF THEISTIC AND CHRISTIAN BELIEF. By Prof. GEORGE P. FISHER, D.D., LL.D. Crown 8vo, $2.50.

FROM THE PREFACE.—"This volume embraces a discussion of the evidences of both natural and revealed religion. Prominence is given to topics having special interest at present from their connection with modern theories and difficulties. The argument of design, and the bearing of evolutionary doctrines on its validity, are fully considered."

JULIUS H. SEELYE, *President of Amherst College.*—"I find it as I should expect it to be, wise and candid, and convincing to an honest mind."

PROF. JAMES O. MURRAY, *of Princeton College.*—"It is eminently fitted to meet the honest doubts of some of our best young men. Its fairness and candor, its learning and ability in argument, its thorough handling of modern objections—all these qualities fit it for such a service, and a great service it is."

ESSAYS ON THE SUPERNATURAL ORIGIN OF CHRISTIANITY. By Prof. GEORGE P. FISHER, D.D., LL.D. 8vo, new and enlarged edition, $2.50.

THE NEW YORK TRIBUNE.—"His volume evinces rare versatility of intellect, with a scholarship no less sound and judicious in its tone and extensive in its attainments than it is modest in its pretensions."

THE BRITISH QUARTERLY REVIEW.—"We know not where the student will find a more satisfactory guide in relation to the great questions which have grown up between the friends of the Christian revelation and the most able of its assailants, within the memory of the present generation."

SCRIBNER'S TEXT-BOOK CATALOGUE.

THE PHILOSOPHIC BASIS OF THEISM. An Examination of the Personality of Man, to Ascertain his Capacity to Know and Serve God, and the Validity of the Principle Underlying the Defence of Theism. By SAMUEL HARRIS, D.D., LL.D., Professor of Systematic Theology in Yale College. 8vo, $3.50.

Dr. Harris embodies in his work the results of his long meditation on the highest themes, and his long discussion and presentation of these truths in the class-room. His fundamental positions are thoroughly in harmony with soundest modern thought and most trustworthy modern knowledge.

THE INDEPENDENT.—"It is rare that a work, which is of necessity, so severely metaphysical in both topics and treatment, is so enlivened by the varied contributions of a widely cultivated mind from a liberal course of reading. His passionate and candid argument cannot fail to command the respect of any antagonist of the Atheistic or Agnostic schools, who will take the pains to read his criticisms or to review his argument. In respect to coolness and dignity and self-possession, his work is an excellent model for scientists, metaphysicians, and theologians of every complexion."

THE HARTFORD COURANT.—"Professor Harris' horizon-lines are uncontracted. His survey of the entire realm he traverses is accurate, patient, and considerate. No objections are evaded. No conclusions are reached by saltatory movements. The utmost fairness and candor characterize his discussions. No more thoroughly scientific work in plan or method or spirit has been done in our time. On almost every page one meets with evidences of a wide and reflective reading, not only of philosophy, but of poetry and fiction as well, which enriches and illumines the whole course of thought."

THE SELF-REVELATION OF GOD. By SAMUEL HARRIS, D.D., LL.D., Professor of Systematic Theology in Yale College. 8vo, $3.50.

In this volume Dr. Harris presents a statement of the evidence of the existence of God, and of the reality of His revelation of Himself in the experience or consciousness of men, and the verification of the same by His further revelation of Himself in the constitution and ongoing of the universe, and in Christ.

PROF. WM. G. T. SHEDD, D.D., in *The Presbyterian Review.*—"Such a work is not brought out in a day, but is the growth of years of professional study and reflection. Few books on apologetics have been recently produced that will be more influential and formative upon the mind of the theological or philosophical student, or more useful. It is calculated to influence opinions, and to influence them truthfully, seriously, and strongly."

BISHOP HURST, in *The Northwestern Christian Advocate.*—"We do not know a better work among recent publications than this one for building up old hopes and giving a new strength to one's faith. The book is thoroughly evangelic, fresh, and well wrought out. It is a valuable contribution to our American theology."

CHRISTIAN EVIDENCES AND HOMILETICS.

THE THEORY OF PREACHING; or, Lectures on Homiletics. By Professor AUSTIN PHELPS. 8vo, $2.50.

This work is the growth of more than thirty years' practical experience in teaching. The writings of a master of style, of broad and catholic mind are always fascinating; in the present case the wealth of appropriate and pointed illustration renders this doubly the case.

THE NEW YORK CHRISTIAN ADVOCATE.—"Ministers of all denominations and of all degrees of experience will rejoice in it as a veritable mine of wisdom."

THE INDEPENDENT.—"The volume is to be commended to young men as a superb example of the art in which it aims to instruct them."

THE WATCHMAN.—"The reading of it is a mental tonic. The preacher cannot but feel often his heart burning within him under its influence. We could wish it might be in the hands of every theological student and of every pastor."

MEN AND BOOKS; OR, STUDIES IN HOMILETICS. Lectures Introductory to the "Theory of Preaching." By Professor AUSTIN PHELPS, D.D. Crown 8vo, $2.00.

Professor Phelps' second volume of lectures is devoted to a discussion of the sources of culture and power in the profession of the pulpit, its power to absorb and appropriate to its own uses the world of real life in the present, and the world of the past, as it lives in books.

PROFESSOR GEORGE P. FISHER.—"It is a *live* book, animated as well as sound and instructive, in which conventionalities are brushed aside, and the author goes straight to the marrow of the subject. No minister can read it without being waked up to a higher conception of the possibilities of his calling."

BOSTON WATCHMAN.—"We are sure that no minister or candidate for the ministry can read it without profit. It is a tonic for one's mind to read a book so laden with thought and suggestion, and written in a style so fresh, strong, and bracing."

A TREATISE ON HOMILETICS AND PASTORAL THEOLOGY. By W. G. T. SHEDD, D.D. Crown 8vo, $2.50.

In this work, treating of the main points of Homiletics and Pastoral Theology, the author handles his subject in a masterly manner, and displays much original and highly suggestive thought. The Homiletical part is especially valuable to ministers and those in training for the ministry. Dr. Shedd's style is a model of purity, simplicity and strength.

THE NEW YORK EVANGELIST.—"We cannot but regard it as, on the whole, the very best production of the kind with which we are acquainted. The topics discussed are of the first importance to every minister of Christ engaged in active service, and their discussion is conducted by earnestness as well as ability, and in a style which for clear, vigorous, and unexceptionable English, is itself a model."

THE CHRISTIAN INTELLIGENCER.—"The ablest book on the subject which the generation has produced."

SCRIBNER'S TEXT-BOOK CATALOGUE.

A MANUAL OF NATURAL THEOLOGY. By GEORGE P. FISHER, D.D., LL.D., Professor of Ecclesiastical History in Yale University. 16mo, 75 cents.

This book carries out an original purpose of Professor Fisher to prepare a manual of Natural Theology, should that on Christian Evidences prove acceptable and useful. It is excellently adapted to class-room use by reason of its concise statements and the natural arrangement of the arguments. Brief definitions, with a statement of erroneous theories and of the place of argument on the subject, comprise the introductory chapter on the Nature and Origin of Religion. The succeeding chapters take up The Cosmological Argument of the Being of God, The Argument of Design, The Moral Argument, The Intuition of the Infinite and Absolute, Anti-Theistic Theories, The Future Life of the Soul; and there is a note upon the Ontological Argument. The division into chapters, with minor subjects indicated by side-headings, makes the volume very convenient for class-room use.

BISHOP VINCENT.—"It is literally *multum in parvo*. It is a good pocket-book for the old student and a good text-book for the young."

THE EXAMINER.—"It would be difficult to find in anything like the same space so complete an outline of the subject. As a text-book in schools and colleges it has merits so obvious and surpassing that it will surely displace other manuals of the kind."

THE CONGREGATIONALIST.—"He has discussed the subject with that profound learning, analytical skill, and literary grace of which he is an acknowledged master; and the high value of his work will be conceded immediately and permanently."

ADVANCE.—"Clear and solid and convincing."

PRESIDENT CHARLES F. THWING.—"This exposition is so clear, succinct, and forcible that it should help to restore natural theology in its proper place in our plan of education."

THEISM. Being the Baird Lecture for 1876. By ROBERT FLINT, Corresponding Member of the Institute of France, Honorary Member of the Royal Society of Palermo, Professor in the University of Edinburgh, etc. Seventh edition, revised. 12mo, $1.50 net.

CONTENTS: Issues Involved in the Question "Whence and How We Get the Idea of God?—Comparison of Polytheism and Pantheism With Theism—Three Great Theistic Religions Compared—Nature, Condition, and Limits of Theistic Proof—Nature But the Name for an Effect Whose Cause is God—The Argument From Order and Objections to It—Moral Argument—Testimony of Conscience and History—Consideration of Objections to Divine Wisdom, Benevolence, and Justice—A Priori Theistic Proof.

CHURCH HISTORY.

BERNARD OF CLAIRVAUX: The Times, the Man, and his Work. An Historical Study in Eight Lectures. By RICHARD S. STORRS. 8vo, $2.50.

THE BEGINNINGS OF CHRISTIANITY. With a View of the State of the Roman World at the Birth of Christ. By GEORGE P. FISHER, D.D., LL.D., Professor of Church History in Yale College. 8vo, $2.50.

THE BOSTON ADVERTISER.—"Prof. Fisher has displayed in this, as in his previous published writings, that catholicity and that calm judicial quality of mind which are so indispensable to a true historical critic."

THE EXAMINER.—"The volume is not a dry repetition of well-known facts. It bears the marks of original research. Every page glows with freshness of material and choiceness of diction."

THE EVANGELIST.—"The volume contains an amount of information that makes it one of the most useful of treatises for a student in philosophy and theology, and must secure for it a place in his library as a standard authority."

HISTORY OF THE CHRISTIAN CHURCH. By GEORGE P. FISHER, D.D., LL.D., Professor of Ecclesiastical History in Yale University. 8vo, with numerous maps, $3.50.

This work is in several respects notable. It gives an able presentation of the subject in a single volume, thus supplying the need of a complete and at the same time condensed survey of Church History. It will also be found much broader and more comprehensive than other books of the kind.

HON. GEORGE BANCROFT.—"I have to tell you of the pride and delight with which I have examined your rich and most instructive volume. As an American, let me thank you for producing a work so honorable to the country."

REV. R. S. STORRS, D.D.—"I am surprised that the author has been able to put such multitudes of facts, with analysis of opinions, definitions of tendencies, and concise personal sketches, into a narrative at once so graceful, graphic, and compact."

PROF. ALEXANDER V. G. ALLEN, *Episcopal Divinity School, Cambridge, Mass.*—"It has the merit of being eminently readable, its conclusions rest on the widest research and the latest and best scholarship, it keeps a just sense of proportion in the treatment of topics, it is written in the interest of Christianity as a whole and not of any sect or church, it is so entirely impartial that it is not easy to discern the author's sympathies or his denominational attitude, and it has the great advantage of dwelling at due length upon English and American Church history. In short, it is a work which no one but a long and successful teacher of Church History could have produced."

SCRIBNER'S TEXT-BOOK CATALOGUE.

THE LIFE OF OUR LORD UPON THE EARTH. By Rev. SAMUEL J. ANDREWS. Considered in its Historical, Chronological, and Geographical Relations. New and revised edition from new plates, with maps and plans. Crown 8vo, $2.50.

The continued demand for this book shows that it meets a want not otherwise adequately met. While it deals with the life of the Lord on earth in its chronological, topographical, and historical relations especially, the work offers far more than a harmony of the Gospels, valuable as that is, since here the skeleton harmony is filled out with all the life and logic of daily walk and conversation. The elements of time and place are discussed as important toward convincing men of Christ's earthly existence and giving a distinct picture of His labors, His outward circumstances, His relations to those about Him.

In the matter of chronology, this work is unquestionably of the first and highest authority, and this revised edition presents the results of the latest investigation and discovery.

THE CHURCHMAN.—"There will not soon be any which can take its place."

THE SUNDAY SCHOOL TIMES.—"Indispensable to the ever-growing class of real students."

EVANGELIST.—"Should be in every minister's library."

CHRISTIAN ETHICS. By NEWMAN SMYTH, D.D., New Haven. [See MENTAL and MORAL SCIENCE.]

HISTORY OF THE JEWISH PEOPLE IN THE TIME OF OUR LORD. By Dr. EMIL SCHÜRER, Professor of Theology in the University of Giessen. Translated from the second edition (revised throughout and greatly enlarged) of History of the New Testament Time.

Heretofore issued in parts, but now complete in a form convenient for general readers. First division. 2 vols. Political History of Palestine from B.C. 175, to A.D. 135. Second division. 3 vols. Internal Condition of Palestine, and of the Jewish People in the time of Christ. With Index to the entire work, in all 5 vols., 8vo., net, $8.00. Single volumes supplied only in the English edition at $3.00 per volume and $1.50 additional for the Index.

Examines into and describes that realm of thought and history in which the universal religion of Christ grew up. The surroundings, prevalent tendencies of thought, spiritual and intellectual life, and the extensive, varied literature of the time, are among the treasures set forth.

ENGLISH CHURCHMAN.—"Under Professor Schürer's guidance, we are enabled to a large extent to construct a social and political frame-work for the Gospel History, and to set it in such a light as to see new evidences of the truthfulness of that history and of its contemporaneousness.

. . The length of our notice shows our estimate of the value of his work."

BRITISH QUARTERLY REVIEW.—"As a hand-book for the study of the New Testament, the work is invaluable and unique."

STANDARD TEXT BOOKS.

HISTORY OF THE CHRISTIAN CHURCH. By PHILIP SCHAFF, D.D. New Edition, re-written and enlarged. Vol. I.—Apostolic Christianity, A.D. 1—100. Vol. II.—Ante-Nicene Christianity, A.D. 100—325. Vol. III.—Nicene and Post-Nicene Christianity, A.D. 311—600. Vol. IV.—Mediæval Christianity, A.D. 590—1073. 8vo, price per vol., $4.00.

This work is extremely comprehensive. All subjects that properly belong to a complete sketch are treated, including the history of Christian art, hymnology, accounts of the lives and chief works of the Fathers of the Church, etc. The great theological, christological, and anthropological controversies of the period are duly sketched; and in all the details of history the organizing hand of a master is distinctly seen, shaping the mass of materials into order and system.

PROF. GEO. P. FISHER, *of Yale College.*—"Dr. Schaff has thoroughly and successfully accomplished his task. The volumes are replete with evidences of a careful study of the original sources and of an extraordinary and, we might say, unsurpassed acquaintance with the modern literature—German, French, and English—in the department of ecclesiastical history. They are equally marked by a fair-minded, conscientious spirit, as well as by a lucid, animated mode of presentation."

PROF. ROSWELL D. HITCHCOCK, D.D.—"In no other single work of its kind with which I am acquainted will students and general readers find so much to instruct and interest them."

DR. JUL. MULLER, *of Halle.*—"It is the only history of the first six centuries which truly satisfies the wants of the present age. It is rich in results of original investigation."

HISTORY OF THE CHURCH OF CHRIST, IN CHRONOLOGICAL TABLES. A Synchronistic View of the Events, Characteristics, and Culture of each period, including the History of Polity, Worship, Literature, and Doctrines, together with two Supplementary Tables upon the Church in America; and an Appendix, containing the series of Councils, Popes, Patriarchs, and other Bishops, and a full Index. By the late **HENRY B. SMITH, D.D.**, Professor in the Union Theological Seminary of the City of New York. Revised Edition. Folio, $5.00.

REV. DR. W. G. T. SHEDD.—"Prof. Smith's Historical Tables are the best that I know of in any language. In preparing such a work, with so much care and research, Prof. Smith has furnished to the student an apparatus that will be of life-long service to him"

REV. DR. WILLIAM ADAMS.—"The labor expended upon such a work is immense, and its accuracy and completeness do honor to the research and scholarship of its author, and are an invaluable acquisition to our literature."

LECTURES ON THE HISTORY OF THE JEWISH CHURCH. By ARTHUR PENRHYN STANLEY, D.D. With Maps and Plans. New Edition from New Plates, with the author's latest revision. Part I.—From Abraham to Samuel. Part II.—From Samuel to the Captivity. Part III.—From the Captivity to the Christian Era. Three vols., 12mo (sold separately), each $2.00.

The same—Westminster Edition. Three vols., 8vo (sold in sets only), per set, $9.00.

LECTURES ON THE HISTORY OF THE EASTERN CHURCH. With an introduction on the Study of Ecclesiastical History. By ARTHUR PENRHYN STANLEY, D.D. New Edition from New Plates. 12mo, $2.00.

LECTURES ON THE HISTORY OF THE CHURCH OF SCOTLAND. By ARTHUR PENRHYN STANLEY, D.D. 8vo, $1.50.

In all that concerns the external characteristics of the scenes and persons described, Dr. Stanley is entirely at home. His books are not dry records of historic events, but animated pictures of historic scenes and of the actors in them, while the human motives and aspects of events are brought out in bold and full relief.

THE LONDON CRITIC.—"Earnest, eloquent, learned, with a style that is never monotonous, but luring through its eloquence, the lectures will maintain his fame as author, scholar, and divine. We could point out many passages that glow with a true poetic fire, but there are hundreds pictorially rich and poetically true. The reader experiences no weariness, for in every page and paragraph there is something to engage the mind and refresh the soul."

THE NEW ENGLANDER.—"We have first to express our admiration of the grace and graphic beauty of his style. The felicitous discrimination in the use of language which appears on every page is especially required on these topics, where the author's position might so easily be mistaken through an unguarded statement. Dr. Stanley is possessed of the prime quality of an historical student and writer—namely, the historical feeling, or sense, by which conditions of life and types of character, remote from our present experience, are vividly conceived of and truly appreciated."

THE N. Y. TIMES.—"The Old Testament History is here presented as it never was presented before; with so much clearness, elegance of style, and historic and literary illustration, not to speak of learning and calmness of judgment, that not theologians alone, but also cultivated readers generally, are drawn to its pages. In point of style it takes rank with Macaulay's History and the best chapters of Froude."

CHURCH HISTORY.

LECTURES ON MEDIÆVAL CHURCH HISTORY. By RICHARD C. TRENCH, D.D., Archbishop of Dublin. 8vo, $3.00.

In this work the author discusses the more important epochs of Church History, tracing the origin and growth of various sects and sketching the careers of the great Schoolmen and Reformers. Introducing his subject with a general consideration of the study of Church History, he devotes his early chapters to the beginning of the Middle Ages, the Holy Roman Empire, the conversion of England and Germany, Monasticism and the Crusades, with accounts of the Mendicant Orders and the Waldenses. His later chapters treat of the great councils of the West, Wiclif, Hus, and their followers, with a view of Christian art, life, and work down to the eve of the Reformation.

THE CONFLICT OF CHRISTIANITY WITH HEATHENISM. By Dr. GERHARD UHLHORN. Translated by Prof. Egbert C. Smyth and Rev. C. J. H. Ropes. Crown 8vo, $2.50.

This volume describes with extraordinary vividness and spirit the religious and moral condition of the Pagan world, the rise and spread of Christianity, its conflict with heathenism, and its final victory.

THE BOSTON ADVERTISER.—"It is easy to see why this volume is so highly esteemed. It is systematic, thorough, and concise. But its power is in the wide mental vision and well-balanced imagination of the author, which enable him to re-construct the scenes of ancient history. An exceptional clearness and force mark his style."

THE SUNDAY-SCHOOL TIMES.—"One might read many books without obtaining more than a fraction of the profitable information here conveyed, and he might search a long time before finding one which would so thoroughly fix his attention and command his interest"

A HISTORY OF CHRISTIAN DOCTRINE. By W. G. T. SHEDD, Professor of Systematic Theology in Union Theological Seminary. 2 vols., 8vo, $5.00.

The work is divided into seven books : 1.—The Influence of Philosophical Systems ; 2.—History of Apologies ; 3.—History of Theology; 4.—History of Anthropology ; 5.—Of Soteriology ; 6.—Of Eschatology ; 7.—Of Symbols. The style is lucid and penetrating, the discussions move onward according to the law of the subjects themselves, as evoked in history ; and new light is thrown on past thought by pertinent illustration from subsequent times.

THE NORTH AMERICAN REVIEW.—"Dr. Shedd has furnished an important contribution to the study of Church history. It is eminently a readable book, and will, no doubt, be extensively read beyond the circle of his own profession by intelligent laymen in all walks of life."

THE N. Y. EVENING POST.—"A body of theological history which is in form as perfect as it is in substance excellent."

BIBLICAL STUDY.

INTERNATIONAL THEOLOGICAL LIBRARY.

Edited by Prof. CHARLES A. BRIGGS, D.D., of Union Theological Seminary, New York, and Prof. S. D. F. SALMOND, D.D., of Aberdeen, Scotland.

This library, undertaken by Messrs. Charles Scribner's Sons in connection with Messrs. T. & T. Clark, of Edinburgh, is designed to cover the whole field of Christian Theology, each volume being complete in itself and yet part of an organic whole. It is to be a series of text-books for students of Theology, and yet a systematic exposition of the several departments of theological science for all intelligent persons. The library is international, interconfessional, catholic, and scientific. The authors have been chosen for their eminent ability in the departments assigned to them. The volumes following are in preparation:

THE LITERATURE OF THE OLD TESTAMENT. By Prof. S. R. DRIVER, D.D., Canon of Christ Church, Oxford. 600 pages, crown 8vo, $2.50 net. New and revised.

An account of the contents and structure of the several books, with some indication of their general character and aim. The origin of the books and the growth of the Canon, according to the Jews, are discussed in an Introduction. Analysis of the Hexateuch (Genesis-Joshua) furnishes the student systematic views of the theme and plan of each book, after which the character and date of the Prophetic and the Priestly narratives are discussed, and a synopsis given of the priest's code. The whole Old Testament is similarly analyzed. Legislative, prophetic, and poetical books are described somewhat more fully.

PROF. WILLIS J. BEECHER, AUBURN THEOLOGICAL SEMINARY.—"While my opinions differ widely from his, I am delighted with the book. It is a full and compact presentation of the views now held by many able scholars. Alike for them and for their opponents it is desirable to have just such a clear presentation of the matter placed within reach."

A HISTORY OF CHRISTIANITY IN THE APOSTOLIC AGE.

By ARTHUR C. McGIFFERT, D.D., Professor of Church History, Union Theological Seminary, New York. $2.50 net.

DR. LYMAN ABBOTT.—"Dr. McGiffert seems to me to have taken away the veil which has so long obscured the Apostle Paul, and to have made his teaching clear and luminous."

CHRISTIAN INSTITUTIONS.

By A. V. G. ALLEN, D.D., Episcopal Divinity School, Cambridge, Mass. 8vo, $2.50 net.

THE PRESBYTERIAN.—"It is absorbingly interesting and contains much information that is very valuable."

BIBLICAL STUDY.

CHRISTIAN ETHICS. By NEWMAN SMYTH, D.D., New Haven.

"The science of living according to Christianity; a comprehensive survey, from the moral point of view, of the founding, up-building, and promised completion of the kingdom of God on earth."

After an introduction on the Nature of Christian Ethics, with its relation to other subjects, the work falls under two grand divisions, as follows: PART I. THE CHRISTIAN IDEAL. Revelation of—Contents of—Realization of—Forms to be Realized—Methods of the Realization—Spheres in which it is to be Realized. PART II. CHRISTIAN DUTIES. Conscience—Duties towards Self—Towards Others—The Social Problem—Duties towards God—The Christian Moral Motive Power.

APOLOGETICS; Or, Christianity Defensively Stated. By ALEXANDER BALMAIN BRUCE, D.D., Professor of Apologetics and New Testament Exegesis, Free Church College, Glasgow. $2.50 net.

Professor Bruce's work is not an abstract treatise on Apologetics, but an apologetic presentation of the Christian faith, with reference to whatever in our intellectual environment makes faith difficult at the present time. It addresses itself to men whose sympathies are with Christianity, and discusses the topics of pressing concern, the burning questions of the time, and is offered as an aid to faith rather than a buttress of received belief and an armory of weapons for the orthodox defender of the faith.

HISTORY OF CHRISTIAN DOCTRINE. By GEORGE P. FISHER, D.D., Titus Street Professor of Ecclesiastical History in Yale University. Crown 8vo, $2.50 net.

One of the most important and eagerly looked for volumes among those announced in the International Theological Library has been the work on the History of Christian Doctrine, by Prof. George P. Fisher, of Yale University. This work is the fruit of many years of study and experience in instruction in this branch of Church History. It comprises not only an account of the rise of dogmas which make up the established creeds, but, also, of the course of theological thought and discussion from the foundation of the Church until the present time. It includes thus a comprehensive survey of modern theology in the Protestant and Roman Catholic bodies, with a clear statement of the influence exerted by the philosophical and scientific researches and theories of recent times.

SCRIBNER'S TEXT-BOOK CATALOGUE.

STUDENTS' NEW TESTAMENT HAND-BOOK. By MARVIN R. VINCENT, D.D., Professor of Sacred Literature in Union Theological Seminary, New York. 8vo, $1.50 net.

The first division of this book—"The Field of New Testament Study"—contains a compact statement of the topics of study and of the best sources of information.

Under the head of "The Criticism of the Canon" will be found a brief history of the development of New Testament criticism from the close of the fourth century to the present.

Under the head of "The Criticism of the Canon in Detail" and under each New Testament book are exhibited the points of controversy raised by the book, the names and opinions of the leading disputants, and the present attitude of criticism.

The second division consists of a catalogue of the best helps to the critical exegesis of the text.

THE CONGREGATIONALIST.—"It is something for which to be grateful."

THE CHURCHMAN.—"It will be found indispensable to all students of the New Testament. We can heartily recommend it."

BIBLICAL STUDY. Its Principles, Methods, and History. By CHARLES A. BRIGGS, D.D., Professor of Hebrew and Cognate Languages in Union Theological Seminary. Crown 8vo, $2.50.

The author has aimed to present a guide to Biblical Study for the intelligent layman as well as the theological student and minister of the Gospel. At the same time a sketch of the entire history of each department of Biblical Study has been given, the stages of its development are traced, the normal is discriminated from the abnormal, and the whole is rooted in the methods of Christ and His Apostles.

THE BOSTON ADVERTISER.—"The principles, methods, and history of Biblical study are very fully considered, and it is one of the best works of its kind in the language, if not the only book wherein the modern methods of the study of the Bible are entered into, apart from direct theological teaching."

THE LONDON SPECTATOR.—"Dr. Briggs' book is one of much value, not the less to be esteemed because of the moderate compass into which its mass of information has been compressed."

MESSIANIC PROPHECY. The Prediction of the Fulfilment of Redemption through the Messiah. A Critical Study of the Messianic Passages of the Old Testament in the Order of their Development. By CHARLES A. BRIGGS, D.D., Professor of Hebrew and the Cognate Languages in the Union Theological Seminary. Crown 8vo, $2.50.

In this work the author develops and traces "the prediction of the fulfilment of redemption through the Messiah" through the whole series of Messianic passages and prophecies in the Old Testament. Beginning with the first vague intimations of the great central thought of redemption he arrays one prophecy after another; indicating clearly the general condition, mental and spiritual, out of which each prophecy arises; noting the gradual widening, deepening, and clarification of the prophecy as it is developed from one prophet to another to the end of the Old Testament canon.

THE LONDON ACADEMY.—"His new book on Messianic Prophecy is a worthy companion to his indispensable text-book on Biblical study. He has produced the first English text-book on the subject of Messianic Prophecy which a modern teacher can use."

THE EVANGELIST.—"Messianic Prophecy is a subject of no common interest, and this book is no ordinary book. It is, on the contrary, a work of the very first order; the ripe product of years of study upon the highest themes. It is exegesis in a master-hand."

THE BEGINNINGS OF HISTORY. According to the Bible and the Traditions of the Oriental Peoples. From the Creation of Man to the Deluge. By FRANCOIS LENORMANT, Professor of Archæology at the National Library of France, etc. (Translated from the Second French Edition). With an introduction by Francis Brown, Associate Professor in Biblical Philology, Union Theological Seminary. 12mo, $2.50.

THE NEW ENGLANDER.—"Mr. Lenormant is not only a believer in revelation, but a devout confessor of what came by Moses; as well as of what came by Christ. In this explanation of Chaldean, Babylonian, Assyrian and Phenician tradition, he discloses a prodigality of thought and skill allied to great variety of pursuit, and diligent manipulation of what he has secured."

THE NEW YORK TRIBUNE.—"The work is one that deserves to be studied by all students of ancient history, and in particular by ministers of the Gospel, whose office requires them to interpret the Scriptures, and who ought not to be ignorant of the latest and most interesting contribution of science to the elucidation of the sacred volume."

QUOTATIONS IN THE NEW TESTAMENT. By C. H. TOY, D.D., Professor of Hebrew in Harvard University. 8vo, $3.50.

THE CONGREGATIONALIST.—"Textual points are considered carefully, and ample and accurate indexes complete the work. The minute and patient thoroughness of his examination of passages and the clear and compact arrangement of his views render his book remarkable. The difficulties of his task were great and he has shown rare skill and has attained noteworthy success in meeting them."

THE CHRISTIAN EVANGELIST.—"Prof. Toy's collection and comparison of the passages quoted in the New and Old Testament is a fine, scholarly piece of work. It surpasses anything that has been done by European scholarship in this field."

SCRIBNER'S TEXT-BOOK CATALOGUE.

THE CHALDEAN ACCOUNT OF GENESIS. By GEORGE SMITH, of the Department of Oriental Antiquities, British Museum. A New Edition, revised and corrected (with additions), by A. H. Sayce. 8vo, $3.00.

THE DOCTRINE OF SACRED SCRIPTURE. A Critical, Historical, and Dogmatic Inquiry into the Origin and Nature of the Old and New Testaments. By GEORGE T. LADD, D.D., Professor of Mental and Moral Philosophy in Yale College. 2 vols., 8vo, $7.00.

J. HENRY THAYER, D.D.—"It is the most elaborate, erudite, judicious discussion of the doctrine of Scripture, in its various aspects, with which I am acquainted. I have no hesitation in saying that, for enabling a young minister to present views alike wise and reverent respecting the nature and use of Sacred Scripture, nay, for giving him in general a *Biblical* outlook upon Christian theology, both in its theoretical and its practical relations, the faithful study of this thorough, candid, scholarly work will be worth to him as much as half the studies of his seminary course."

GEORGE P. FISHER, D.D., LL.D.—"Professor Ladd's work is from the pen of an able and trained scholar, candid in spirit and thorough in his researches. It is so comprehensive in its plan, so complete in the presentation of facts, and so closely related to 'the burning questions' of the day, that it cannot fail to enlist the attention of all earnest students of theology."

WORD STUDIES IN THE NEW TESTAMENT. By MARVIN R. VINCENT, D.D. Vol. I.—The Synoptic Gospels, Acts of the Apostles, and the Epistles of Peter, James, and Jude. Vol. II.—The Writings of John. Vol. III.—The Epistles of Paul. 8vo, per vol., $4.00.

The purpose of the author is to enable the English reader and student to get at the original force, meaning, and color of the significant words and phrases as used by the different writers. An introduction to the comments upon each book sets forth in compact form what is known about the author—how, where, with what object, and with what peculiarities of style he wrote. Dr. Vincent has gathered from all sources and put in an easily comprehended form a great quantity of information of much value to the critical expert as well as to the studious layman who wishes to get at the real spirit of the Greek text.

REV. DR. HOWARD CROSBY.—"Dr. Vincent's 'Word Studies in the New Testament' is a delicious book. As a Greek scholar, a clear thinker, a logical reasoner, a master in English, and a devout sympathizer with the truths of revelation, Dr. Vincent is just the man to interest and edify the Church with such a work as this. There are few scholars who, to such a degree as Dr. Vincent, mingle scholarly attainment with aptness to impart knowledge in attractive form. All Bible-readers should enjoy and profit by these delightful 'Word Studies.'"

BIBLICAL STUDY.

THEOLOGICAL PROPÆDEUTIC. A General Introduction to the Study of Theology, Exegetical, Historical, Systematic, and Practical, including Encyclopædia, Methodology, and Bibliography. By PHILIP SCHAFF, D.D., LL.D., Professor of Church History in Union Theological Seminary, New York. 8vo, 600 pages, $3.00 net.

This book is intended to be a guide for theological students. It gives an outline of the various departments of theology, defines their nature and aim, their boundary lines and organic connection, their respective functions and value; it sketches their history, and indicates the best methods of prosecuting their study. It is the first original work on *Propædeutic* in America.

J. HENRY THAYER, *Divinity School of Harvard University.*—"It exhibits his well-known skill in clear, concise, interesting statement and his wide bibliographical knowledge."

PROFESSOR C. D. HARTRANFT, *Hartford Theological Seminary.*—"It must have a high mission in shaping theological science in our land, as so many of your undertakings have done."

J. PACKARD, *Dean of the Episcopal Theological Seminary of Virginia.*—"We therefore hail this work as supplying a *desideratum* in our course of theological study, and we hope it may be introduced into every theological seminary in our country."

THE EVANGELIST.—"The most satisfactory book in print for the guidance and orientation of the theological student in his first seminary year."

THE SCIENCE OF RELIGION. (Gifford Lectures.)

By C. P. TIELE, Dr. Theol., Professor of the History of Religions in the University of Leyden. 2 vols. Crown 8vo, $2.00 net each. Vol. I. now ready.

CONTENTS: Conception, Aim, and Method of the Science of Religion—Conception of the Development of Religion—Stages of Development—The Lowest Nature-Religions—Stages of Development—The Highest Nature-Religions—Stages of Development—The Ethical Religions—Directions of Development—Directions of Development in Particular Religions and in Groups of Kindred Religions—Laws of Development—Influence of the Individual in the Development of Religion—Essentials of the Development of Religion.

CONTEMPORARY THEOLOGY AND THEISM.

By R. M. WENLEY. 12mo, $1.25.

CUMBERLAND PRESBYTERIAN.—"Dr. Wenley's style is remarkable for swiftness and force, his logic is keen, his analytic faculty strikingly good, and, in fact, his treatment of the entire subject unique in interest and importance."

SYSTEMATIC THEOLOGY.

SYSTEMATIC THEOLOGY. By CHARLES HODGE, D.D., LL.D., late of Princeton Theological Seminary. New Edition, complete in three volumes, including index. 8vo, $8.00 net.

In these volumes are comprised the results of the life-long labors and investigations of one of the most eminent theologians of the day. The work covers the ground usually occupied by treatises on Systematic Theology, and adopts the commonly received divisions of the subject: Vol. I.—Theology; Vol. II.—Anthropology; Vol. III.—Soteriology and Eschatology. The Introduction is devoted to the consideration of method, or the principles which should guide the student of theology, and the different theories as to the source and standard of our knowledge of divine things, Rationalism, Mysticism, the Roman Catholic doctrine of the Rule of Faith, and the Protestant doctrine on that subject.

The plan of the author is to state and vindicate the teachings of the Bible, and to examine the antagonistic doctrines of different classes of theologians.

The various topics are discussed with that close and keen analytical and logical power, combined with that simplicity, lucidity, and strength of style which have already given Dr. Hodge a world-wide reputation as a controversialist and writer, and as an investigator of the great theological problems of the day.

THE SUNDAY-SCHOOL TIMES.—"It is perhaps not too much to say of it, that this is the most important contribution to the literature of theology made since the days of Jonathan Edwards. The reputation of Dr. Hodge in this department, by reason of his life-long associations and his eminent abilities, is such as to command for him, as a recognized authority, respectful hearing in all the churches."

THE NEW YORK CHRISTIAN ADVOCATE.—"This volume is a monument of thought and Christian scholarship, and will be welcomed and studied by intelligent minds in all the Christian denominations."

QUESTIONS ON THE TEXT OF THE SYSTEMATIC THEOLOGY of Dr. Charles Hodge, together with an exhibition of various schemes illustrating the principles of theological construction. By A. A. HODGE, late Professor in Princeton Theological Seminary. 8vo, paper, $1.00 net.

The questions contained in this volume are designed to assist the student in the analysis of the text, and in fixing the points to be grasped by his understanding and retained in his memory, and further for the use of the professor during review and examination.

SYSTEMATIC THEOLOGY.

DOGMATIC THEOLOGY. By WILLIAM G. T. SHEDD, D.D., Professor of Systematic Theology. 2 vols., 8vo, $7.00.

CHRISTIAN INTELLIGENCER.—"The publication of a System of Theology by Prof. Shedd marks an epoch in scientific religious thought. His training has been such as to fit him exceptionally for this culminating work. A great charm in these bulky volumes is the beautifully clear, precise, and simple style in which they are written. The layman can read them with as much ease and interest as the professional theologian."

JOHN DE WITT, in *Presbyterian Review.*—"It is didactic rather than polemic. He states, expounds, and defends what he believes to be the true view, and spends little time in expounding and opposing heresies. The discussions are compact. The style is absolutely clear."

NEW YORK EXAMINER.—"The two volumes are the result of eighteen years of special study and of forty years' labor in theological research. The treatment is such as might be expected of Dr. Shedd: scholarly, devout, profound, thorough."

PRACTICAL THEOLOGY. A Manual for Theological Students. By J. J. VAN OOSTERZEE, D.D., Professor of Theology in the University of Utrecht. Translated and adapted to the use of English readers by Maurice J. Evans. 8vo, $3.50.

This is the result of instruction in practical theology, given by the author during a period of fifteen years at the University of Utrecht, but its original form has been modified or supplemented to adapt it more completely for use as a text-book. As an additional feature of interest the historic portion of the work contains such brief notices of our leading Anglo-Saxon preachers, Christian poets, and catechists, as seemed necessary to furnish the connecting link in English Church History between the movements of the Reformation age and those of our own day, and to make evident the unbroken continuity of the Church's life amidst the constant variation of outward forms.

CHRISTIAN DOGMATICS. A Text-book for Academical Instruction and Private Study. By J. J. VAN OOSTERZEE, D.D., Professor of Theology in the University of Utrecht. Translated by John W. Watson, B.A., and Maurice J. Evans, B.A. Two vols., 8vo, $5.00.

THE PRESBYTERIAN BANNER.—"The volumes before us are a rich mine for the student and the theologian. The arrangement is good, the style clear, and the spirit evidently evangelical. The study of these volumes will stimulate thought, enlarge the vision, and strengthen faith, while they will supply rich material for all whose calling it is to preach the gospel."

THE CHRISTIAN INTELLIGENCER.—"Dr. Van Oosterzee is undoubtedly a ripe and distinguished scholar, and the work before us is his greatest and most successful effort. It has already received high commendation from some of the ablest English scholars, and is certified to by Drs. Smith and Schaff as giving 'the mature results of long-continued, earnest, and devout study of the articles of our Christian faith;' who also add that 'it will prove a safe and useful guide to students in our institutions of learning.'"

SCRIBNER'S TEXT-BOOK CATALOGUE.

GOD'S REVELATIONS OF HIMSELF TO MEN. As successively made in the Patriarchal, Jewish, and Christian Dispensations and the Messianic Kingdom. By Rev. SAMUEL J. ANDREWS. 1 vol., crown 8vo, $2.50.

The object of this book is to set forth historically and doctrinally the manner in which God has revealed Himself to men, His purpose as given in the Scriptures, historical and prophetic, and the high place of the Incarnation in that purpose. The larger part of the book shows that the personal self-revelations of God are in increasing degree as man is obedient to Him. The other sections, Revelations of God in the Christian Church and in the Messianic Kingdom, are more directly concerned with our existing relations to God and to Christ.

NEW YORK EXAMINER.—"We have little hesitation in saying that this book is the most important contribution yet made to the science of Biblical Theology from a pre-millenial point of view. It is certainly the most sober, rational, and consistent presentation of this view that has come to our notice. The work is not polemic; it does not consider objections, or stop to argue with the other side. So far as we have observed, it is quite free from forced interpretations of Scriptures. It should be said, moreover, that it is rich in homiletic suggestions."

THE CHURCHMAN.—"We have left little or no space to speak of the many merits of the volume. Anything that Mr. Andrews writes must be interesting and instructive, and there is much, very much, in this treatise that combines these not always united characteristics."

THE PAULINE THEOLOGY. By GEORGE B. STEVENS, Ph.D., D.D., Professor of New Testament Criticism and Interpretation in Yale University. 8vo, $2.00.

A study of the origin and correlation of the doctrinal teachings of the Apostle Paul. CONTENTS: Conversion of Paul and its Relation to his Mission and Theology—Style—Shaping Forces—Sources of Pauline Doctrine—Doctrine of God—Sin—The Law—The Person of Christ—Doctrine of Redemption—Justification—Christian Life—The Church—Eschatology—Bibliography—Texts—Index.

THE TEACHING OF JESUS. By Prof. HINRICH WENDT, D.D., Ord. Professor of Theology, Heidelberg. Translated by Rev. John Wilson. In two volumes, 8vo. Vol. 1 now ready, $2.50 net. Vol. II. ready soon.

In the belief that a resolute return to the teaching of Jesus Himself will be the most powerful and efficient means of promoting and strengthening the Christian religion in our time, Dr. Wendt seeks to give, in this important work, an authentic, complete, unmixed exposition of the historical elements of the teachings of Jesus.

Of the German edition Prof. J. Iverach said in the *Expositor:* "It is a work of distinguished learning, of great originality, and of profound thought;" and Prof. W. R. Harper calls it "remarkably suggestive, . . . deserving to be ranked among the most important contributions to biblical theology."

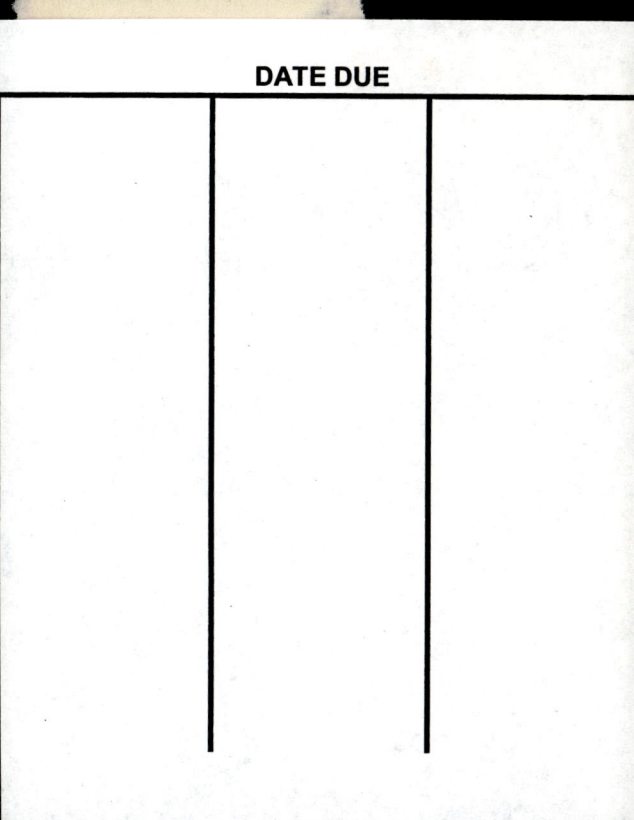

"Let him rather sit still, I said slow."